Magnetic Wealth

Magnetic Wealth

❖

The Six Irrefutable Laws of Prosperity

Dan Rawitch

iUniverse, Inc.
New York Lincoln Shanghai

Magnetic Wealth
The Six Irrefutable Laws of Prosperity

Copyright © 2007 by L Daniel Rawitch

All rights reserved. No part of this book may be used or reproduced by any means, graphic, electronic, or mechanical, including photocopying, recording, taping or by any information storage retrieval system without the written permission of the publisher except in the case of brief quotations embodied in critical articles and reviews.

iUniverse books may be ordered through booksellers or by contacting:

iUniverse
2021 Pine Lake Road, Suite 100
Lincoln, NE 68512
www.iuniverse.com
1-800-Authors (1-800-288-4677)

Because of the dynamic nature of the Internet, any Web addresses or links contained in this book may have changed since publication and may no longer be valid.

The views expressed in this work are solely those of the author and do not necessarily reflect the views of the publisher, and the publisher hereby disclaims any responsibility for them.

ISBN: 978-0-595-45448-8 (pbk)
ISBN: 978-0-595-89760-5 (ebk)

Printed in the United States of America

Contents

Introduction . . . . *vii*

Chapter 1   You've Been Deceived 1

Chapter 2   It Really Does Work 11

Chapter 3   What if I bonked you on the Head? 23

Chapter 4   The Irrefutable Law of Attraction 29

Chapter 5   The Irrefutable Law of Emotion 43

Chapter 6   The Irrefutable Law of Focus 52

Chapter 7   The Irrefutable Law of Gratitude 60

Chapter 8   The Irrefutable Law of intention 68

Chapter 9   The Irrefutable Law of Least Effort 76

Chapter 10 Putting it all together 87

Conclusion 95

Introduction

I am not a big fan of long introductions. In fact, I often skip them and like to get right to the meat of the book. Just in case you are anything like me, I will keep this introduction short and to the point.

First and most importantly, thank you for purchasing my book! I have spent my life learning how to find peace, happiness and prosperity. While I believe life is a journey and I still have long to travel before reaching my destination, I have come to understand the Human spirit and through that understanding, I have found happiness.

They say money cannot buy happiness, while I guess that statement is true, as my father always pointed out, "Money cannot buy poverty" either. What I did learn while accumulating wealth and material possessions was that I was not happy because I feared I would loose what I had acquired.

What has made me blissfully happy is the knowledge that I create my own life. The empowerment that has come from this knowledge is priceless! I finally understand how my thoughts and focus shape everything around me. My thoughts shape my job, my relationships and my net worth. When I do not like what I see, I simply change my thoughts and my focus toward what I would like. Happiness always follows this exercise and with happiness comes money.

So, I guess "They" were right! Money does not bring happiness BUT I am CONVINCED that happiness will bring money!

Lastly, I really want to know your thoughts about this book! If you feel you did not receive value from the purchase ... I DO NOT WANT YOUR MONEY!! Please contact me for a full refund. I am convinced that anyone can benefit from these teachings. The wisdom and laws have existed since the beginning of time and everyone I know that practices the Six Laws of Prosperity is both wealthy and happy.

Please share your stories with me! I answer all emails. Also, please sign up for my True Success Ezine, so that we may stay in touch.

All my best,

Dan Rawitch

1

You've Been Deceived

My intention for this book is to change your life! I intend to help you get everything that You want and to help you understand why there may be things lacking in your Life, at this very moment.

There have been countless books written on the subject of "manifesting" your desires. These books can be found in many different sections of your local bookstore. I have found great books in the spiritual, psychology, self-help, and business sections of book-stores. I can honestly say that I have gotten something good out of every single book I have read on the subject of creating affluence. In some of the books I may have picked up only one new idea; other books I have carried with me for years, continually rereading tattered and dog-eared pages. If I purchased a book and disliked the style of writing or if I found the book boring, I did my best to skim the material and search for the one good take-away idea that I knew existed.

Why am I telling you this? Mainly because I want you to understand that I have been a life-long student of success and have literally read hundreds of books on the subject. The Six Irrefutable Laws of Prosperity are a culmination of the wisdom I have garnered from countless masters, as well as from my own incredible experiences.

As you read this material, you may notice repetition in certain areas. You may notice that I find many different ways to say the same thing. I do this intentionally and I have not lost my mind. I believe you must read many of the statements contained in this book many times. The more you subject yourself to this knowledge, the more likely it will penetrate your consciousness and become adopted as your beliefs. I heard it said recently by Jerry Hicks, co-author of *Ask and It Is Given,* that a belief is simply a thought you think about over and over. The information this book will provide you works and hopefully can alter some of your limiting beliefs! Practicing the six laws can and will lead you to a happier and more fulfilled life. Be patient with some of the repetition in the book. My desire is that you allow the words to safely and securely seep into your subconscious. You will love the impact this knowledge will have on your life!

◆   ◆   ◆

All of my reading and studying started when I was nineteen years old and I met an amazing man named Jim Rohn. I was so blown away when I first heard Jim speak that I used my very first credit card to finance his tapes. I still remember the name of the seminar and tapes purchased almost thirty years ago: "Adventures in Achievement." I wish I still had the tapes!

Meeting Jim Rohn

When I was a freshman in college I belonged to the college's Marketing Club. I know that sounds nerdy, but I was a little bit of a nerd! So what! At that time a really cute girl in the club gave me a free ticket to Jim's seminar. Since I had no money and knew for certain this girl would never go out with me, I decided to go to the seminar and pretend it was a date. As I mentioned earlier, I was utterly impressed and captivated when I heard Jim speak. I remember sitting in the large auditorium in San Jose, California, and wondering why on earth my father, a serial entrepreneur, never bothered to tell me any of the amazing information that Jim Rohn was freely rolling off his silver tongue.

I was relatively shy at that age (and still am), but I decided I *had* to get up the nerve to introduce myself to Jim. Although he was busy, he took the time to greet me; he gave me his card and invited me to call him any time. I stared at the card for a number of weeks until the cute girl at school asked me if I had the nerve to do something with it. Not wanting to appear wimpy, I finally convinced myself to dial the number. My call was routed to the manager of Jim's San Jose office. The gentleman warmly invited me to come into the San Jose office the following week, when Jim would be in town.

I ended up working for Jim Rohn in that same office. My job was to promote Jim—sell tickets to his seminars and help market his books and tapes. People who worked for Jim were taught to practice the ideas he taught. One of the key things we all learned was to read, read, and read some more. In fact, for almost thirty years and whenever practical, I have spent at least thirty minutes a night reading things that could better my life. Jim told me to start my life of reading with the book *Think and Grow Rich* by Napoleon Hill. I quickly followed up that *amazing* and magical book with a tiny red book called *It Works*. It was a coincidence that I read those two books back to back; I must say that the combination of the two created immediate wonders in my life.

One Mentor Leads to Another

Jim Rohn was important because his beliefs helped build the original foundation of my personal values and belief systems. Equally as important, Jim Rohn unknowingly led me to my next important teacher.

Anthony Robbins, one of the greatest personal development gurus on the planet, was also trained and taught by Jim Rohn. I mention this because it may be the closest I will ever come to comparing myself to Tony Robbins. I suppose if I have to model myself after somebody, it should be the absolute best there ever was! When I saw the first Tony Robbins infomercial, almost twenty years ago, I made a snap judgment about him and gave him very little credit. The next time I saw the infomercial something about him struck me as being very real and very powerful.

Soon after releasing his tapes, Tony published his wonderful first book, *Awaken the Giant Within*. In the first chapter, he writes about his rough beginnings, including living in a studio apartment and washing dishes in his bathtub. He had almost lost all hope in his life until meeting Jim Rohn. Once I realized Tony had been mentored by the same man who started me on my path, my admiration for Tony grew. I have attended many Tony Robbins events, read his books, and purchased all of his cassette programs. I am also coached by Karen Vice, one of Tony's few, elite coaches in the country.

◆ ◆ ◆

At the outset of my career, I began an interesting pattern of literally going from rags to riches and back to rags again. I created amazing amounts of wealth, drove exotic cars, and lived in six-thousand-square-foot country club mansions; and then, before I knew it, I would begin a financial slide almost all the way back down again.

Oddly, each time I slid back to the bottom, I would immediately start creating wealth again.

At that time I did not put two plus two together and truly believed I was either a fortunate or unfortunate victim of luck. When things were going poorly I would sometimes feel guilty and think perhaps God was punishing me for being greedy and wanting more when things were going well. Ouch! Pretty tough to feel good when things are going well, if you think God is about to smack you back down again! In this book we will discuss exactly who it is who controls your success or failures. I assure you, God has delegated 100 percent of that power directly to you.

You will also learn to share my belief that "luck" does not have a damn thing to do with your financial condition either. I know it sometimes feels that way and I know that it is very often more simple to believe luck is the culprit. Fortunately, luck does not control your destiny. Your destiny is in your hands all of the time; yep, all day, every day, with absolutely no exceptions.

Right now, many of you are shaking your heads and thinking my statements cannot be true. I'll bet you that by the time you finish this book, you will have taken a huge step toward sharing my belief on this issue.

Okay, if I rule out luck and God from the equation, then why would I create wealth only to keep giving it back? The answer is simple: I kept getting exactly what I was focusing on. Each time I made a lot of money, I shifted my focus from wealth creation to wealth protection. The more I thought about protecting what I had, the more fearful I became about losing what I had. It turns out that fear is one of the most attractive forces in nature. I do not mean "attractive" as in "beautiful"! I mean "attractive" like a magnet. Animals can smell fear; dogs will attack when they sense it and man seems to be unconsciously drawn toward it.

The first major clue of this book has just been given: *fear is magnetic!* The more time you spend focused on your fears, the more likely you will attract the very thing you fear into your life! *Wow!* Trust me; I will devote ample pages of this book to explaining exactly why this occurs and exactly how to stop magnetizing your fears.

Back to my question: why did I keep going from riches to rags? The answer, if you have not guessed it yet, was fear. Every time I got a ton of money and a life style that others dream about, I stopped thinking about all the cool stuff I wanted and started thinking about how to keep what I had. Focusing my thoughts on not losing what I had invoked a ton of fear. So much fear that it consumed many of my waking hours. Instead of having fun playing golf, I was doing math in my head, *ugly* math. The kind of math that would assume: the market will crash, expenses will rise, and income will cease. The goal of the math was to attempt to predict how much longer my money would last if every bad thing I was focused on came true.

I do not recommend you try this at home! I can already tell you what will happen. You will go broke and almost exactly when you predict it will happen. How about that?

Let's examine the overall pattern. I start at or near the bottom and begin practicing the amazing things I will teach you. My wealth grows *very* quickly and in ways I cannot even understand. Now from my position the top, I stop doing the things and practicing the beliefs that made me a winner and I start looking down. Oh boy, it looks like a long way to fall from here! No longer concerned with how to get and have more, I become consumed with keeping what I have. Practicing my magic ceases! Hell, I have no time for magic! I am too focused on survival and *fear*—fear that *I* magnetize. Here we go again, back to the bottom.

Once I began to realize the pattern, I became obsessed with how to break it. How can I use the tools that helped get me to the top, to keep me at the top? Finally, after twenty-five years, I understand the secrets well enough to share them. Before getting into the meat of the material, I think it is important to discuss my upbringing and how some of my reverse-programming began.

◆ ◆ ◆

I was lucky enough to grow up in a fairly normal home with loving parents and all the comforts of a middle-class household. I am absolutely convinced my dad always wanted the best for me and intended all the things he taught me and told me to be helpful and educational. In fact, I think he was trying to prepare me for the cold, hard, and unfair world.

This was his first mistake! The world is not cold, hard, or even the slightest bit unfair, unless of course you hold within you a strong belief that it is. We will spend time examining the power of your beliefs later. The whole truth is that my dad's insight into the "cold world" came to him quite accidentally from one of the greatest men I will ever know. I am referring to my grandpa, Grandpa Jack, a man who worked his entire life for low wages as a furrier. A furrier is a person who makes fur coats. My grandpa spent his life in a small backroom with a concrete floor, sewing together pieces of animal fur into coats. Now mind you, back then the public had very few, if any, political opinions and little awareness about the issue of killing small animals for their fur. I suspect if it were known back in those days to be wrong, Grandpa Jack would have found himself another trade.

After many years of making minimum wages working for someone else, Grandpa Jack decided to open a retail store of his own. He put together a lifetime of savings, opened the store, and began enjoying the fruits of his labor. Shortly thereafter, *wham!* The store was broken into and every single thing was stolen. With no insurance, Grandpa Jack was broke. He never complained, he simply packed up the family and moved from Chicago to Los Angeles and began his new life. With no money and few contacts, his new life looked a lot like his old life. Grandpa once again became a furrier working for low wages. The difference between my grandpa and many other people was that he found true peace and happiness in what he did. He was also a very skilled furrier. He bought a nice little home and provided a good life for his family. I believe he became content with what he had and never really wanted more—or believed he could or should have more.

Now enter my father. He hungered for and demanded a grander life style than he was raised with. He had the confidence and belief that he could and should have more and he constantly went after what he wanted. Things seemed to come easy for my dad; the problem was he lived in fear that he would lose everything, as his father had. My dad was cursed with a double whammy. Not only did he fear what he had would be taken away, he also experienced tremendous guilt for what he accumulated. I remember him saying to me many times that he felt guilty for how much more money he made than his father.

With the little information I have already shared with you, I'll bet you can guess where this will lead. Guilt for what he had, multiplied by the fear of losing it, can only lead to one thing. Loss of everything! If fear is a magnet and you combine it with the strong emotion of guilt, the result is quite predictable. Please lock in on this: anything you think about repeatedly will be drawn toward you. If you think about something with strong emotion, it will come even faster.

It seems my dad lived a version of my rags-to-riches life and along the way he unconsciously taught me how to do the very same. Statements like "nothing good ever comes easy," can have a lasting effect on a kid. The good news for my dad is that he learned to control the ups and downs of his life and has retired to a very nice life style. I shudder to think how wealthy my dad would have become if he had understood the Six Irrefutable Laws of Prosperity.

◆　　◆　　◆

After much struggle and because of my growing realization of the Six Irrefutable Laws of Prosperity, I have broken the pattern and live an absolutely amazing life! The best part is I understand where everything I have comes from and how to keep it while accumulating more. By the way, the accumulation of money and material possessions is only part of the real joy that these secrets can teach you. Your new beliefs will also bring you the relationships you have always desired.

Now, it is time to start learning what makes *you* tick. What negative patterns in your life are you ready to shatter? What do you really want in life? What have you been afraid to go after? If you will take a journey through this book with me, I promise you will understand exactly how to have what you want. You will also understand why you do not already have your desires. Open your mind, open your heart, and turn up your imagination because your life is about to get even better!

2

It Really Does Work

The purpose of this chapter is make double sure that I have your complete attention! You must have an open mind about what I will teach you. If I am your tour guide, you must believe I know the territory I am about to lead you through. The only way I know to accomplish this is by sharing personal miracles.

My first real test of the Irrefutable Laws came after reading the book *Think and Grow Rich*. I was twenty-four years old and very clear that I wanted much more out of life. The book was written by Napoleon Hill, a man who dedicated his life to understanding success. He studied and interviewed some of the greatest men this country has ever known, such as Henry Ford, Andrew Carnegie, Thomas Jefferson, and of course Thomas Edison. Hill found that there were several attributes that linked all of these men together. Some of the key ones were desire, clarity about what they desired, strong emotion about having their desire and total faith in the attainment of their desire. The idea being, once you commit yourself to your desires, your subconscious mind will go to work and begin finding ways to bring them to you. Simply stated, focus your energy on what you want and then pay attention to ideas and urges that will come to you.

After reading this book, I felt compelled to read more! I thought I understood what Hill was talking about, but could not quite pull it together in my mind. When I got to the bookstore I was immediately drawn to a tiny book named *It Works*. The book was so small I actually read it while standing in the aisle of the store. I bought the book anyway and went immediately home to begin practicing the teachings. Somehow, this simple book brought to life the information Napoleon Hill was trying to convey.

Without giving away all of the ideas of the book, because I think you should buy it, I'll tell you that I did exactly as suggested by the author. I wrote down what I intended to have and then read the statement several times a day. I then told myself I had planted a seed and convinced myself the seed was growing beneath the ground and soon I would see a sprout. Although after a few weeks I still saw no sprout, I stayed focused on my list with complete faith that the outgrowth of my desires would soon pop its mysterious head out from under the soil.

It happened when I least expected it to happen. I was playing tennis with some friends when the idea hit me. In fact, the idea hit me just after I had tossed the ball in the air to serve. The feeling was powerful enough that I could not serve the ball. Instead, the ball hit ground and bounced at my feet. My friends yelled at me and asked, "What the hell are you doing?" I replied, "I don't know but I think I need to go home." Being a very literal young man, I was not about to ignore Napoleon Hill's advice and let this impulse he promised I would get slip by. I needed to get home and think over this flash from above.

At that time I owned a teeny tiny mortgage brokerage company. It was a tough business and being a mortgage broker in the early eighties was not at all fashionable. The industry did not really take off until the late eighties. Because the industry was still young, it lacked credibility and my company was relegated to working on only the toughest deals that the banks would not do. Consequently, 75 percent of the loans we tried to fund, did not fund. Hence, we only got paid on a minority of the loans we worked on. This was discouraging and made it hard to get ahead financially.

The morning of my tennis game, I recall thinking about how cool it would be if I could figure out a way to get paid on every deal I touched. I could not come up with any legitimate way to accomplish this, so I put it out of my mind. My mind—that is, it seems my subconscious mind—continued to work, even during my tennis match.

As I tossed the ball into the air to serve, I heard myself say, "Credit bureaus get paid on everything they touch." The ball dropped to my feet and I thought about the statement. Every loan I did needed a mortgage credit report and I had to pay up front for every one of them. How hard could it be to start a mortgage credit reporting company? With that question in mind, I said goodbye to my tennis buddies and ran to my car, all the while listening to them swear at me for walking out on our Saturday morning game.

I will spare you the details and tell you that my partner and I figured out a way to start a very small credit reporting company with almost no cash and absolutely no experience, contacts, or knowledge of the business. None of that mattered to me! The idea was too good and I was too convinced it manifested from the focus I put on my list of desires. We named the company Data Fax; it grew to be one of the largest mortgage credit reporting companies in the nation, with multiple offices in multiple states. Prior to selling the company we produced several hundred reports each day, at a cost of forty-dollars each. The company was sold just before my thirtieth birthday, for a price well into the seven figures. Imagine, I woke up to play tennis and went to bed building a multimillion-dollar-a-year company—with no money and no experience.

Dan Wants a Boat

_____If the story of Data Fax did not convince you that what I have to teach you will work, let me tell you about the time I manifested a very big boat. After we sold Data Fax, I started another mortgage company. It too was wildly successful. Although the company was successful, I later found myself in a precarious position. You see, I had always wanted to run a publicly traded company. When the opportunity arose to sell my business to a public company and to be on the board of directors, I jumped at the chance.

Perhaps I jumped too fast! I sold my mortgage business to the public company mostly for shares of stock. Meaning, instead of being paid several million dollars in cash, I accepted several million dollars' worth of stock. At the time of the sale, the stock in the acquiring company was trading at over five dollars per share. In just a few short months, the company that purchased mine had fallen on hard times and the stock price fell dramatically. In fact, the stock fell as low as twelve and one-half cents. Everything that I had worked for was now tied up in worthless stock. It was then that the company sought the resignation of the then—chief executive officer and asked me if I would be willing to become the CEO. Remember earlier I mentioned that I had always wanted to run a public company. I must have focused on this long enough to manifest the desire!

Okay, now I am running a company which has no money and is unable to pay me a salary. I was a little excited and a lot depressed. I knew from my teachings that if I focused on my depression and on the mistake I had made selling my company to the wrong buyer that I would draw failure into my life. I needed to feel happy and draw positive events into my life. For some silly reason, I decided a big boat would make me happy, not just any big boat—it needed to be big enough to live on and have the range to take me directly to Cabo San Lucas, a place that also made me happy.

My wife, always a fantastic supporter, told me, "Sure, honey, if you can figure out how to buy a boat right now, go for it." I think what she was saying without sounding negative was, "If you can buy a boat using your currently worthless shares of stock or make payments on it without a paycheck, go for it."

Armed with the knowledge that I can have anything I am willing to focus passionately on, I decided to get busy. I began purchasing every yachting magazine in publication. I also spent all my spare time at whatever marina I was near. I went to boating shows and I accumulated boating knowledge and terminology. At night, I put myself to sleep imagining I was piloting my boat to Mexico while talking on my satellite phone and doing business. I knew where I wanted to berth my boat and even pictured having parties on the dock with all my best friends. With all the extreme and positive emotional focus on the boat, there were times when I even thought I already had one. At the risk of sounding like a crazy person, I will tell you that I actually became delusional about the boat. One guarantee I can make you is that the moment you find yourself actually believing you have something, it is coming to you in a hurry. I will elaborate more on this later. For now, suffice it to say that I had tricked my subconscious mind into believing I had the boat and by the Law of Attraction, the boat would be delivered.

During this period, a friend of mine had called me to ask me if I could help him purchase a block of stock from a public company in which I knew the CEO. I offered to help him and never gave the conversation another thought. A couple of weeks later, after spending the evening at the Oakland boat show I went to sleep dreaming about my boat. At three o'clock that morning the phone rang and it was the friend I helped to purchase the block of stock. I answered the phone both irritated and groggy. The voice at the other end was cheerful and wide awake. He said, "Good morning, Dan, I have fantastic news for you." I said, "Do you have any freaking idea what time it is?" He said, "Sure, it is 9:00 a.m. here in Monaco." To which I dryly replied, "Well, I'm not in Monaco and I really do not give a damn what time it is in Monaco." He ignored my response and went on to tell me he was walking on the beach with his pants rolled up and the warm water was lapping at his feet. Before I could again let him know I did not give a damn, he informed me he just resold the block of stock I helped him purchase a couple of weeks ago. He went on to tell me he made several million dollars' profit on the transaction. I still didn't care; I wanted to go back to sleep. My friend's last words were, "I am going to do something nice for you."

The next day was the last day of the boat show and I found my dream boat. It looked like a million-dollar boat. She was fifty feet long had two spacious state rooms and was about the most beautiful thing I had ever seen. Although the boat looked brand new, it was about six years old and was selling for $245,000. Not much for a boat like that, but still about $245,000 more than I had at that moment. Remember, I was still holding onto seemingly worthless stock and not collecting a paycheck, while trying to turn around a very troubled company.

I left the boat show somehow knowing I'd found the boat I would own. While focusing my energies on the boat, the phone rang. It was my friend, telling me he was leaving Monaco and flying to San Francisco. He invited me to meet him at the Fairmont Hotel and told me he had a gift for me. In the lobby of the hotel, we visited for a minute and he then handed me a Hermes box. Hermes is a European company famous for making incredible cashmere sweaters and silk scarves. My friend always wore Hermes and I often commented on them. I was so thrilled to be given a very expensive Hermes sweater that I thanked him with a huge smile. He smirked and said, "Oh, I had forgotten how much you admire Hermes." He continued, "If it's Hermes you desired, you may be disappointed." With that, I started to rip open the box. He grabbed my arm and said, "No, not here—open the box when we get to my suite." The moment we entered his room I opened the box. It was not Hermes and I was certainly not disappointed. Inside the box was $250,000—just enough to buy my boat.

I fully believe my intense focus on the boat, which subsequently led my unconscious mind to accept the idea, eventually brought me the exact opportunities necessary to have the boat. Later I will touch on quantum physics, which has proven that if a thought can exist, then the seed to create the thought must also exist. Simply stated, anything can be thought into reality! For now, please let my boat help prove the point. I promise to support this premise with plenty of information.

My Wife Wants a New House

A blissful year of living on the boat had now passed. We named the boat *Angel's Play* for obvious reasons and created a lifetime of memories in just one short year. One morning my wife, Sophia, woke up and said, "I feel seasick." Being the sensitive husband that I am, I laughed at her and said, "How can you be seasick? First of all, you live on a boat, and second of all, we are not at sea. We are sitting on the dock." She looked at me blankly and proceeded to win the argument by throwing up at my feet. I was convinced she was sea sick and we quickly left the boat and headed for higher ground. At that time, we were fortunate to have a home in Incline Village, Lake Tahoe. Our Tahoe home proved to be a perfect place to seek temporary refuge from what turned out to be a typical case of morning sickness.

Although I was elated beyond words about the prospect of being a father, we had some new challenges to overcome. To begin with, my company's corporate office was located in downtown San Francisco and our home was located in Lake Tahoe. At least three and one-half hours separate the two locations—not quite a reasonable commute. The boat, at Pier 39 in San Francisco, was also not an option, due to Sophia's pregnancy. We certainly could not live on the boat after Sophia gave birth to our baby girl, either. We did not want to sell our Tahoe home and my company had yet to complete its turn-around, so its stock price was still too low for me to sell any shares. It was time to get busy attracting and manifesting again.

This time, it was my wife who became delusional. She began home shopping with no cash and in a price range that astounded me. Sophia had always been conservative with money, so the fact that she was shopping for a new home at that point in out lives was surprising.

I will never forget the evening she convinced me to go look at the home that later became ours. I left my office and drove from San

Francisco to Walnut Creek. There was a lot of traffic and we did not arrive until dusk. We parked at the end of a street and I said, "Okay, where is the house?" She pointed almost straight up and said, "Way up at the end of that long, private driveway." She said this with a big smile because she knew I had always visualized having a home at the end of a long, private driveway. I looked up in amazement and said, "Ah, c'mon … you're kidding!" It took a few minutes to convince me to drive up that driveway. Once Sophia informed me the house was vacant and that we were only going to look into the windows, I became sold on at least taking a peek.

Immediately I could see this was the house of my then-current dreams. The structure was sort of country French and the home sat on a hillside with a view to die for. From city lights to the majestic Mount Diablo, we could see everything, completely unobstructed. The view was literally 180 degrees, as the house sat on knoll all by itself. Even more amazing, the house was on over an acre of land, a good portion of which was flat and usable. I should tell you, my fantasy home needed to have a view and a flat lot with a backyard and pool. This home certainly had it all from the outside. While wishing to myself that I could peek at the inside, unbeknownst to me, my wife was running around the entire house trying every door. Of course the very last doorknob she twisted responded by turning and in she went. The next thing I knew, she was standing on the threshold of the back door near where I was standing, with a mischievous grin on her face.

I reluctantly entered the home, feeling like I really should not be in there just as it was getting really dark. As luck (or manifestation) would have it, I flicked a light switch and the lights came on. Something magic happened to us while in the home on that completely dark and quiet night. We must have spent an hour or so just looking at the view and wandering from room to impressive room. A switch clicked in my head and I suddenly saw myself living in that house.

Mind you, we did not have the down payment, and the monthly payment would have been far too great of a strain at that time. I knew from my past manifestations that now more than ever was *not* the time to give any thought as to how I was going to get that home. It simply was not my job to figure it out. My job was to believe and accept that it would be my home. From there, the Law of Attraction and all the other laws I will discuss, would lay out the plan for me.

Each time I found myself doubting whether or not I would own the home I was manifesting, my wife and I would go back up that driveway and sneak back into the door that magically remained unlocked. After several visits to the house, we had mentally placed all the furniture, picked out which room would be the nursery, and even planned our first party. Later you will learn just how important this step is to the final process.

One night while wandering through the house that we had again snuck into, we heard a car quietly winding up the quarter-mile private driveway. My heart stopped and I thought for sure I was headed to jail for breaking and entering. There was no way out; even if we could get to our car, we could never get down the driveway without being seen. There was room for only one car in each direction. We sheepishly walked to the front porch to confront our visitor.

When the door opened to the large black Mercedes, which had just pulled into the driveway, I mustered up the warmest smile I could and said, "Welcome to my dream house!" The driver got out smiled and said, "Oh, so you're the culprit?" He went on to explain that the one of the neighbors had been repeatedly calling and telling him that there were people spending countless hours in the home, which he, as the real estate agent, had listed. I pled guilty and apologized. The realtor simply smiled and said, "You must *really* love this house." I told him just how much we loved it and explained our entire situation, including the fact that I could not buy the house until my stock price went up to at least five dollars per share. I explained that I was committed to not selling any shares until that point. I also explained that my stockbroker would not let me borrow on the stock until it hit the five-dollar mark. The realtor (I will call him "Bob") asked us to keep him posted on the share price and to let him know when we were ready to make an offer. I acknowledged that I would, and he promised to call us if it looked like anyone else was interested in the house.

Once again, the Law of Attraction had put us in the right place at the right time! It turns out we made such an impression on Bob that he called the owner of the home and told him about us. The owner had just sold a company for over forty million dollars, allowing him to purchase a winery and estate in Napa. He was busily investing his new fortune in real estate and the stock market at the time Bob called him. The owner of the home became very intrigued with my company and inquired about what the NASDAQ symbol for our shares was.

A week or so went by. We then got a call from Bob, who informed us that the owner of the home was fascinated by my stock and would like to buy shares directly from me instead of from his broker. I explained I was unwilling to sell stock below five dollars, but thanked him for the offer. A couple of days later we received a call directly from the owner of the home. He asked if we would meet him at the home and expressed an interest in knowing more about my company. Within five minutes of meeting us, his wife said, "They're the ones; they must live in this home." It was sort of weird, but then again, not really, when you understand the Six Irrefutable Laws of Prosperity.

My wife and I were of course bewildered, so the owner went on to explain that their home was very special to them; in fact, they considered it to be almost a magic house. It seems their daughter was born in the home, their business was built from scratch in the home, and that they too, leveraged themselves into it ten years ago. They were very committed to putting just the right buyers into their previous dream house.

"Mr. Seller" went on to tell me that he believed my stock price would blow through five dollars and that I would be stupid to sell it for anything less than eight dollars. So convinced was he, that he invited us to move into the home and not worry about making a down payment until the stock hit the eight-dollar mark.

What on earth are the odds that we would find our dream home where all of these circumstances existed? I am either the luckiest guy on the planet *or* the Irrefutable Laws work. If you choose to think I am lucky, you are wrong and I will convince you otherwise!

Within ninety days of moving into our new home, the stock did indeed blow through five dollars; it also blew through eight dollars and ten dollars before hitting a peak price of sixteen dollars. We ended up selling a substantial amount of shares at twelve-fifty, the exact number I began manifesting exactly three years prior. I will share this story later when I begin detailing the Six Laws for you. Even as I write this story and recall the events of 1999, I am still amazed at the power of the Six Laws!

3

What if I bonked you on the Head?

Several years ago, I gave a speech at one of my company events. During my talk, I asked five people to volunteer and join me on the stage. As they walked onto the speaker's platform, I asked them to line up, facing sideways to the audience. I informed them that I knew a magic spell and that every time I cast my spell on someone, their life would immediately begin changing for the better. Some people looked at me as if I were a complete lunatic; others smiled while telling themselves I was kidding; and the third group watched in amazement, wondering if I did possess such power.

I then began rubbing my heads feverishly together while repeating the following words, "I, Dan Rawitch, do hereby call upon the almighty powers of the universe. I ask the infinite intelligence that provided electricity through Jefferson, light through Edison, and flight through the Wright Brothers, flow freely and powerfully through me, around me, and from me. I also call in every subatomic particle necessary to attract every positive thing these five people desire. I ask that these particles of pure energy become magnetized with the proper vibration to align these individuals with their most intense desires. All they need do now and for the rest of their lives is to state their desires with passion; and through that passion and focus, all of their dreams will come true. To guarantee this process, I hereby invoke the Law of Attraction, the Law of Least Effort, and the Law of Intention. So be it,"

Now, you have to picture me chanting these words with passion. Each word grew louder and stronger as I paced back and forth on the stage, rubbing my hands together like a madman. When I finished the incantation, my hands were hot from the friction of being rubbed together. I walked up to each of the five individuals and gently slapped my open palm against his or her forehead, just as you may have seen an evangelical healer do on television. They felt the heat of my palm and the very slight sting of my slap and opened their eyes looking extremely bewildered. I stared each one down with a deliberately and well-rehearsed deranged face. I did not speak; there was complete silence in the room. I waited to see which of the five would speak first. I knew that the reaction of the first person could potentially influence the feelings of the other four. It did not matter to me what the reaction was—I had a point to make either way.

The first to speak was a man in his early twenties. We will call him Greg. He was the only one of the group who would not make direct eye contact with me. When he finally looked at me and spoke, he began laughing hysterically, causing the other four and the entire audience to laugh. When Greg stopped laughing, I asked him if he had felt anything at all while listening to my words. He replied "No," and then admitted he had cheated and opened his eyes while I was chanting my spell. Because he had been sneaking a peek at my stage act, he simply could not take me seriously. Clearly, Greg felt nothing and did not even really listen to the words I said.

Next, a woman in her early forties spoke up. We will call her "Connie." She was much more confident in her eye contact and said she found the words I chanted to be powerful and that they gave her chills. Connie never opened her eyes and had no idea I was being a goofball on stage. She went so far as to say that when I touched her, she felt a rush of energy run through her body. I looked at Connie and admitted that each time I use the incantation I had just used on her; I too get a chill and feel a rush of energy. I looked at the audience and asked, "What if this really works?"

What if this prayer, incantation, or affirmation really worked on Connie? What would your life be like if I could cast the same spell on you? What if you completely believed, at that moment, that your entire life just changed for the better and that you could have or do anything you desired? How would you behave? How would you walk or talk? What things would you buy? How would you begin relating to your coworkers or your boss? Would you start that new business? Would you take a day off from worrying about your bills? I wonder if you would finally plan that vacation or buy that engagement ring. Really, what would you do if I could cast a magic spell on you? I am convinced that if you believed and acted as if this spell were really cast upon you, your life would never be the same! As we cover the Six Irrefutable Laws of Prosperity, you will understand that gaining prosperity can really be as simple as a bonk on the head.

Let's examine how Greg reacted after he left my speech. I am guessing he told his friends I was funny and informative. I doubt he told them he'd just witnessed a life-changing event and I doubt he did anything different that day. We can most likely agree that Greg was completely unaffected by the event.

Okay, now let's talk about Connie. She thought she felt something shift within her and I think she well may have. Will this event help her gain prosperity? Connie now has a partial picture in her mind that her life may actually get better. Can she hold onto the picture of a better life? The challenge most people face is that the picture they attempt to hold is too fluid and they cannot hold onto it. If Connie walked out of the auditorium and found her car sitting in the parking lot with a new big dent in it, I can bet she would immediately let go of the positive picture I painted for her. She would most likely say to herself that Greg was right and go on with her day.

But what would happen if Connie walked out of the auditorium and there was a business card on her windshield? Let's imagine the card was from an old friend and coworker she lost touch with five years ago. On the back of the card was written, "I cannot believe you still have this car and that I found you." Connie immediately dials her friend's number and is amazed to learn her former coworker is now CEO of a large software company. She offers Connie a great job paying more money and with stock options. Connie would immediately tell herself that my magic spell really worked and she would begin acting as if her life had changed.

Either of the two imaginary outcomes was possible. I have personally had both of those two things happen to me. My point is that anything is possible and we cannot ever control external events in our life. The only thing we can control is how we react to external events. Connie walked away from her encounter with me, thinking maybe I zapped her with some positive energy. She could choose to hang onto that feeling or let it go. Most likely, the events following my speech will help her decide whether something good happened to her or not. You will soon learn that the Law of Attraction will attract other thoughts, opportunities, and events that match up with her current thoughts. If Connie felt positive, she would attract positive events. If she decided to let the dent in her car change her feelings, she would reverse the process and begin attracting negative events. The trick is that we need to hold our positive thoughts long enough for them to manifest, or bring about something.

What all this means is you need to continue holding your positive focus and your desires until you see positive results. Unfortunately, the easy thing to do is to stop your positive focus as soon as an external event occurs that does not make you happy. I like to think about this as a movie in which your mind is the projector and the world is your screen. When I want something I project the picture of the exact thing I want—let's say it's a new boat—onto my life's screen. I keep the picture burning bright regardless of what external events are showing up for me. If I project the picture of my new boat and then get met with bad news, like a pay cut or an unplanned expense, I will not allow the news to change my picture. If I did, then I would be reversing the process. I would be allowing the world to be the projector and my mind would be the screen. Once I let the world project its pictures upon my mind, I become a victim of any external event that shows up. I urge you to be the projector! Remember, you cannot control external events. You *can* control what you choose to focus on and how you choose to react. Soon you will become convinced that you get what your projector focuses on.

Before we begin covering the Six Irrefutable Laws of Prosperity, please allow me to again infuse you with my magic words. Please read these words at least three times. When you finish reading all six of the prosperity laws, you will then understand the complete meaning of these words.

> I do hereby call upon the almighty powers of the universe. I ask the Infinite intelligence that provided electricity through Jefferson, light through Edison and flight through the Wright Brothers to flow freely and powerfully through me, around me, and from me. I also call in the subatomic particles necessary to attract the positive things I desire. I ask that these particles of energy become magnetized with the proper vibration to align themselves with my greatest desires. All I need do now and for the rest of my life is to state my desires with passion. Through my passion and focus, all of my dreams will come true. To guarantee this process, I hereby invoke the Law of Attraction, the Law of Least Effort and the Law of Intention. So be it.

Have you repeated the above affirmation three times? You need not understand the magic of these words to have them work for you. If you have read them three times with passion and excitement, you should feel positive. Now, in this positive state, briefly close your eyes and think about something you desire. It is helpful to visualize your desire as well as think about it. Remember, you are projecting the picture of what you want onto the screen of the world. This picture cast from a positive state of mind will begin drawing the events necessary to attract the object of your desire.

There, I gave you my magic words and bonked you on the head. Take the magic and run with it toward everything you ever dreamed of.

4

The Irrefutable Law of Attraction

I have begun with the Law of Attraction because I believe it to be the most important of the six laws. Entire books have been written on this subject alone. In many ways the Law of Attraction includes the other five laws and can very much stand on its own as a primary driver for your success. The premise is simple but not always easy to follow. Many of us still struggle with staying true to this law, even after we fully understand its power. You will know you have mastered the Law of Attraction when you become aware of all of your thoughts. Once aware of your thoughts, you can begin the vital process of shifting them toward your desires.

The easiest way to think about the Law of Attraction is to think about your mind as a magnet, a very powerful magnet that can draw to you events and circumstances that match your polarity. I have used the image of a radio station to help me visualize the Law of Attraction. When I tune my frequency to a certain channel, I will pick up the station that is broadcast to that channel. In other words, if my mind is tuned to rock and roll, I certainly will not pick up a jazz station. By the same token, if my mind is tuned to problems and negativity, I will not pick up opportunities or positive events.

Have you ever awakened in the morning and had everything go wrong? You can't find anything to wear, you get shampoo in your eyes, and the coffee maker won't work. I think most of us have had a version of a morning like this. Does it normally end there? Most of the time, this is just the beginning. We get in the car and it needs gas. We get to the gas station and the pump won't work. When we finally get on the freeway, we are confronted with bumper-to-bumper traffic. I can assure you right now, you are emitting a bad signal or frequency. If you do not shift your focus away from your terrible morning, the problems will carry through to your work environment. When you have a morning like this, have you noticed how rudely everyone seems to treat you? You cannot get waited on in the restaurant. The bank teller ignores you and the dry cleaner loses your favorite shirt. Why do these bad things keep piling on top of one another?

Sadly, we experience the same piling on of problems on a more macro basis as well. Sometimes bad events and circumstances continue through long cycles. Have you ever had your life take a sudden turn for the worse? One day things look pretty good and the next day things start getting bad. Maybe it starts with some bad news in the mail, perhaps a tax audit or something annoying like that. The next day you get some bad news at work only to come home that evening to a busted water pipe and the news that your dog's run away. So far, I am talking about things that probably have happened to all us at one time or another. For some of us, these things I just mentioned are only the beginning. Sometimes downturns lead to terrible struggles. Why is that?

Once again, you are emitting a bad frequency and attracting bad events. The first key to the Law of Attraction is awareness. The moment I catch myself attracting a bad morning, I immediately start focusing on things that I desire. I start thinking about all the good things in my life and imagine the perfect day. I continue this intense shift in focus until I feel good again. Magically, as soon as I start feeling good again, things turn around and start falling back into place.

So far, I have only touched on the effects of the Law of Attraction. Now I would like to give you a much deeper understanding. However I caution you, the Law of Attraction is always working for you or against you whether you understand it or not. You do not have to believe in the concept either. The Law of Attraction is an irrefutable law of the universe.

I recently watched the movie *The Secret* (which I highly recommend). In the movie, Bob Proctor compared the Law of Attraction to electricity. He explained that he did not understand how electricity worked but he still enjoyed all of the benefits it provided him. He went on to make his point by saying, "Electricity can cook a man's dinner and it can also cook the man." This is a brilliant way to look at the Law of Attraction. You do not need to fully understand it but you should indeed understand that it affects your every waking moment. We should use the law to cook our desires and not cook ourselves by attracting what we don't want!

We should begin with a basic understanding of quantum physics. Trust me, I only have a basic understanding of the subject and I will not profess to be an authority on the topic. What I have learned from quantum physics is that absolutely everything in the universe is made up of energy. It is fascinating to understand that everything is made of exactly the same stuff. I am talking about oak trees, rocks, flowers, skin, human organs, metal, and anything else you can possibly think of. If you were to take a powerful enough microscope and examine the inside of an acorn, you would see it is made up of exactly the same stuff that your hand is made of; your hand is made of the same stuff as rock or a car. Just what is beneath the surface of all these items? It begins with molecules. Heck, you remember that from high school, right? Inside the molecules you find protons, neutrons, and atoms. This should be sounding a little familiar from your school days. Do you know what is inside an atom? Pure energy; in fact, enough energy to light a city. This energy comes from subatomic particles that vibrate at incredible speeds. These particles never stop moving. They are so small that we have yet to invent a microscope powerful enough to see them. The only way we know these subatomic particles exist is because we have invented high-powered microscopes that can see the trails the particles leave behind.

This concept gets very advanced and can almost start sounding like science fiction. If you want to learn more, I would recommend reading Deepak Chopra's book, *Creating Affluence*. I am going to gloss over some amazing facts about subatomic particles because after years of reading about quantum physics, I still feel like a madman when I start going into too much detail. I have told you enough to make a point and draw out the relevance to the Law of Attraction. Now that you know everything is made of the same stuff, you should also know this includes your brain and your thoughts. Scientists can measure a thought and have proven it has a frequency. The funny thing about energy and the subatomic particles that make up energy is that they are always on the move. Energy will also only travel to places containing the same vibrations. When you send a thought from your brain, you have summoned countless subatomic particles containing enough energy to literally create your thought.

Whoa! You had better stop and think about that for a minute. The implications are fantastic! Napoleon Hill said this fifty years ago. He said, "Thoughts are things." I only wish I could have really understood that when I first read his book twenty-five years ago. Hopefully, with brief understanding of quantum physics and how energy is made up, you will not have to wait as long to grasp the concept. Remember what I said: "When you send a thought from your brain, you have summoned countless subatomic particles containing enough energy to literally create your thought."

Understanding and practicing this concept is good news and will make your dreams come true. Ignoring this will lead you to continue to live your life in exactly the same patterns you have always experienced. Imagine for a moment what millions of subatomic particles might look like. I like to picture them as tiny flashes of white light or dots. These particles, or energy if you will, are always in a hurry. They are very literal and have no sense of right, wrong, or your personal reality.

Amazingly, each particle contains intelligence. In fact, all energy contains intelligence. When you think hard about something, the particles are on their way to you. The problem that I mentioned earlier is that most of us cannot hold a thought long enough to accept the delivery. If I wake up in the morning thinking about and wishing for a new car, within a nano-second, the particles are on their way. If on my way to work, I start thinking about my bills, I have tuned away from the vibration or frequency of the particles and away they go to find a new vibrational match somewhere else.

That is only a small part of the bad news! The real bad news is that I just put out a new thought, a powerful one routed in fear and scarcity. The new thought is about having too many bills. This new negative vibration has just placed an order for countless new subatomic particles. Only these new little buggers are going to bring you more bills. Remember, whatever you focus your thoughts on must grow! It is an irrefutable law of nature. Think about bills and more will come. Think about a car and one will come.

I suppose this is good news and bad news. Imagine how frightening it would be if you immediately manifested everything you thought about. What if you thought about lions and then opened your eyes to find one in bed with you? I do not think any of us would want things to come that fast. The whole trick is that you have to hold your focus long enough to create a strong emotion around that which you desire. Think about the boat I created. I thought about boats, I read about boats, and I went to boat shows. I continually summoned the energy to me to create my boat. I did not care how I would get the boat and I had no idea how it would come to me. I knew that the Law of Attraction would illuminate the path for me. I knew that circumstances and events would begin to surface that ultimately lead to my owning a boat. That is how it works.

I will say again, the problem most people face is that they cannot hold their focus long enough for the appropriate amount of subatomic particles and energy to gather around them and manifest their desires.

Did you know that if you burn metal—which of course is made of energy and in fact is one of nature's elements—that the smoke from the metal you burn will only be attracted to the smoke of the same metal? In other words, if I burn gold at one end of the room and silver at the other end of the room, the smoke from the two metals will repel each other. They have different energies. If I burn gold, copper, and silver at one end of the room and the same three metals at the other end of the room, the smoke from each metal will find its vibrational match somewhere in the room. Gold will go to gold, silver will go to silver, and copper will go to copper. Like energy attracts like energy. We have all heard some of these sayings: "like attracts like," "birds of a feather flock together," and "misery loves company." I suspect someone has been trying to tell us these things for a very long time.

More, Please

Years ago, I manifested my first plane. The plane was a 1980 Piper Saratoga, a plane which I could easily afford because of how old it was. The challenge was that I was in no way qualified to fly a high-performance, six-seat airplane. Even if I personally felt qualified to fly this plane, it would have been impossible for me to get insurance. I had not flown in many years and needed to update my skills, my medical certificate, and my confidence. Being the impulsive person that I am, I began plane shopping long before I even knew how I could fly one home. I was highly confident I would find a way, even though I had chewed up and spit out three consecutive flight instructors. I needed to find an instructor who would match up to my personality, understand my learning pace, and most importantly have a very flexible schedule. Also, my new instructor would himself need to be qualified to fly my plane.

The reason this was all so important was that the insurance company would require me to have at least one hundred to two hundred hours of hands-on instruction before they would allow me to be the pilot in command of a high-performance, complex airplane. Believe it or not, most flight school instructors have only logged hours in the small, low-performance planes owned by the schools they teach for.

About the day I found my plane, I met Scott. He was perfect in every way. Scott had recently left a successful career to follow his dream of flying. He was in his mid-thirties, much more mature than most of the other flight school instructors, who were barely old enough to drive. Scott also had the experience and hours required to fly my plane and he was a CFII-level instructor. Equally as important, I enjoyed his company, my family trusted him, and we could all see ourselves spending several months with Scott sitting in the front right seat of our new plane.

Even though my first plane was nineteen years old, she was the most beautiful thing I had ever seen. I was ignorant as to what really mattered about a plane at that time in my life, so I focused on the paint and interior. I had to have bling! The paint job was very unusual—navy blue and silver. She also had plush navy blue leather with blue carpet, configured as club seating with a total of six seats. Not too bad for a first plane!

The day we went to pick her up was one of the most exciting days of my life. The plane was hangered on an island in Washington State; the only way to get to the island was by private plane. My wife, Scott, and I flew into SeaTac Airport in Seattle. The seller of the plane, Andre, agreed to fly into SeaTac in his new plane, pick us up, and fly us to the San Juan Islands, where my new Saratoga would be waiting. Can you imagine how exciting this was? At the time, I was forty years old and had fantasized about this moment for my entire life!

When Andre landed, my jaw dropped. I watched him touch down in his brand-new plane and could not believe my eyes. Andre was selling me his old Piper Saratoga because he had moved up to a new Piper Malibu. The Malibu was the sexiest plane I had ever seen. Don't worry—Andre's Malibu did not detract at all from the excitement I was feeling for the purchase of his old plane. Scott climbed into the copilot seat of the Malibu while my wife and I climbed into the spacious rear cabin. The Malibu is a fully pressurized cabin-class airplane. Heck, it even has three stairs to climb up into the cabin.

The moment we got comfortable, my wife casually made a remark that caused a whole bunch of brand-new subatomic particles to head our way. She reclined in one of the roomy backseats of Andre's plane and said, "Now, this is a real airplane." As soon as the words escaped her mouth she looked into my eyes and said, "Oops!" She then said, "Dan, I know that look—please give it time." She was right. Although I was excited beyond imagination to take delivery of my new Saratoga, at that moment it became very clear that I would one day own a Malibu Mirage. As always, there was a thing or two to overcome. First, I would need well over five hundred hours as pilot in command; second, I would need to spend over a million dollars for the new plane.

When you become proficient at using the Law of Attraction, at times you can actually feel something shift inside of you when you lock into something you are attracting. I think it about like a tractor beam from *Startrek*. Remember when a Klingon ship would lock the *Enterprise* into their tractor beam? Once something was locked into the beam, it was going to end up in the belly of the Klingon ship. This is a great visualization to practice when you are manifesting something. I picture the tractor beam as a ray of light coming from me and locking onto the target of my desire; in my imagination, the ray of light is made up of millions of brightly lit subatomic particles. Later I will discuss how vital imagination is to the attraction process. There are scientific reasons why imagining things can make them real.

Meanwhile, let's go back to airplanes for a minute. I knew when I sat in the rear cabin of that Piper Mirage that I had just begun manifesting a new plane. It may seem crazy, since I had not even taken delivery of my first plane! To some this could sound ungrateful or unappreciative toward the plane I was about to get. Trust me; I was incredibly appreciative and grateful! I will be devoting an entire chapter to gratitude. After reading the chapter on gratitude, you will realize that gratitude is a foundation of success and I am grateful for *everything* I have.

I am convinced that life has greater meaning when we have something in our sights (or tractor beam). When we stop wanting more, we risk becoming complacent. Complacency can lead us to wanting to protect what we have and protection will lead to fear. I discussed in chapter 1 the frustrating pattern I put myself and my family through when I was younger. Each time I accumulated wealth, I became complacent and then fearful. Once I began focusing on my fear of losing everything, the Law of Attraction kicked in and I indeed would lose everything. An interesting point about energy is that it is always expanding or contracting. It never sits still and it never stays the same. Because everything in the universe is made up of energy, this means that everything is either expanding or contracting. Another way to look at this is that everything in the universe is either growing or dying. Think about plants, trees, and animals. Everything is always growing or decaying. How about you? Would you rather be constantly in an expansion or a contraction mode? I vote for expansion! That is why, on the day I purchased one plane, I already had selected my next plane. Two years later, I purchased my third airplane. As you would expect, the new plane was a Malibu.

After purchasing the Malibu, I immediately put another plane into my tractor beam. My fourth plane will be a huge step up and will take some serious manifestation to create. Recently I decided it is time to get busy, so I have really kicked in the turbo chargers and begun the attraction process. I will discuss with you exactly how I am managing this process. If you are willing to follow the steps I will detail for you, I believe you can obtain anything you desire.

Attraction Exercise

1. *Pick your target*—this should be something you want very badly and that you can actually see yourself possessing.

2. *Visualize your target*—See *all* aspects of that which you plan on acquiring. You should be able to clearly visualize the goal. When I started practicing the Law of Attraction, I was at a slight disadvantage because I did not think in visual pictures. I have since trained my mind to *see* my intentions as well as *think* them. I will give you a hint: if

you cannot see your goal, it may be too big for you. In other words, you yourself may not think the goal is attainable.

3. *Put your target in the tractor beam and see it coming toward you*—You will find if you continue this exercise, you will actually see the target coming closer to you with each visualization session.

4. *Practice*—Practice step three a minimum of twice daily.

5. *Begin paying careful attention to any hunches that develop*—When I turned up the attraction burners for a new plane last month, things began to develop quickly for me. First, I was asked to give a speech at a mortgage banking event. The hired speaker had to cancel at the last minute and they needed me to fill in. During that speech, I detailed my some of my thoughts on the Law of Attraction. After my talk, a woman approached me and said, "You have obviously seen the movie *The Secret!*" I told her I had heard of the movie, but had yet to see it. She encouraged me to see the movie and asked if I would give a presentation to her company. She went on to suggest that I combine the teachings of the *Secret* with my personal experiences and knowledge, speculating that people could benefit from such a seminar.

Okay, this was interesting but still no light bulb had gone off for me. At night, while visualizing my new plane, her suggestion continued to play in my mind. I reminded myself that I was in the middle of manifesting and decided to pay closer attention to the idea. The next day, our former nanny and friend came by to visit my daughter. She handed the *Secret* to me and demanded I watch it while she took my daughter to lunch. It was midday on a Saturday, and although my wife and I had plenty to do, we decided we needed to watch the movie.

After watching, I was hooked and immediately went to their website, www.thesecret.tv, and began surfing around. There are several smart, congruent, and informative speakers in the movie who present key aspects of the secret itself. The website provides background information on each of these experts and links to their websites. Bob Proctor, whom I mentioned earlier, offers from his website to send out daily inspirational messages. He promises not to give out his members' email addresses but does keep you posted of events he is interested in.

A few days later, I received an email from Proctor's website informing me of an event that Mark Victor Hansen, the co-author of the *Chicken Soup for the Soul* books, would be putting on. The event was to be a three-day seminar, packed with the some of the world's greatest speakers, all willing to teach the five hundred or so attendees how to build a speaking business.

When I received the invitation to attend the event, the light bulb really did go off for me! I have been helping people for years become more successful. I have been an unpaid speaker hundreds of times. I am writing a book and I love to speak to large groups. Duh ... why not begin giving paid speeches around the country and promote my new book? If Mark Victor Hanson is willing to give me a lifetime of knowledge as to how he and others have built their speaking empires, I sure as heck am willing to listen. I am certain to my very core that people will benefit from what I have to say. The only thing missing for me was how to get my message to the masses and promote myself as a speaker. I knew that these questions would be answered for me at the speakers' seminar.

Can you see how one seemingly unimportant event led to another? On their own, each event meant almost nothing to me and no light bulb went off. Because I was in the midst of manifesting, I had asked the Law of Attraction to lead me down the appropriate path. My job was simply to follow the path. None of these events or ideas was forced, none of them required any effort, and in the end they will lead me to yet another income stream. My income will be positively impacted by this new venture. More importantly, as I move toward a national speaking tour, *I need to have a bigger and faster plane.* Just watch how this plays out!

6. Never think about *how* you will get the object of your desire! Wondering or worrying about "how?" is the fastest way I know to drive your desires away from you and out of your tractor beam. Thinking about "how?" is the number one killer of all manifestations. Asking "how?" will invoke fear; and fear is the enemy of what you are attracting. Fear will only attract itself. I have several exercises for eliminating "The Hows."

My favorite exercise is to immediately and intensely form a picture of what I want and see it in my tractor beam coming toward me. I will not release that picture until the question of "how can I have it?" goes away. The universe will show you how, just pay attention! In the movie *The Secret,* Jack Canfield gave a great analogy. He explained that when we drive our car at night, our headlights only illuminate a couple hundred feet in front of us. We cannot see our destination and cannot even see the next mile. This does not stop us from getting to our destination. All we really need to see is one hundred feet at a time. The universe will show you the next hundred feet of your journey if you pay attention.

Remember, we are dealing with quantum physics and the irrefutable Law of Attraction. The events and circumstances necessary to bring you what you are attracting will unfold 100 percent of the time. You just have to stay focused on your desire and pay attention to your hunches.

If you will follow these steps with faith and passion, you will be amazed how quickly that which you desire comes to you. Please continue focusing on what you want until it comes to you. Stopping the process is the only way to fail! Do not become one of the many who quit just before their greatest dreams come to fruition. You have planted a seed; do not dig it up to see if it is growing, Trust that the irrefutable Law of Attraction will deliver and the seed of your desire will grow to fruition.

5

The Irrefutable Law of Emotion

If you want to know if the Law of Attraction is working for you, simply notice how you are feeling. If you want to know if the law is working against you, also notice how you are feeling. The Law of Attraction is always either working for you or against you. It is never neutral and the law never sits idle.

Your life will change immediately when you start paying attention to the fact that you will attract whatever you are feeling! Sadly, most of the population is ignorant of this reality. The Law of Attraction will always seek out and find a vibrational energy match to whatever you are feeling. In previous chapters I wrote that you will attract what you are focusing on or thinking about. Although what I wrote was accurate, it contained only part of the truth. You see, thoughts come and go in fleeting seconds and at times are hard to notice or even control. Some would say we cannot control our thoughts at all.

A thought is only the first step toward the attraction process. When we hold a thought for more than a couple of seconds, it becomes our focus. When we focus on something, it will gradually change how we feel and create an emotion. Quite simply, if you focus on a happy thought for a few seconds, you will begin to feel happy. Try it right now: think about something that would make you happy. I often think about my youngest daughter's smiling face or my Bull Dogs under bite, with his lower teeth sticking up over his upper lip. Sometimes I think about my nineteen-year-old daughter in her new sorority house on the campus of UC—Davis. I am so proud of her and I know how much fun she is having in college. These thoughts cannot help but make me feel happy. Have you come up with your happy thought yet? If you have, I would like you to focus on it for a minute or two. If you are really focusing on something that makes you happy, you cannot help feeling happy,

The same is true if you think about something that makes you unhappy. You do not have to try it; just take my word for it! I want you stay happy! Allow me to review this simple progression.

1. A thought pops into your head
2. You decide to focus on that thought
3. Your emotion shifts according to the thought *you chose* to focus on!

Why is this information important? The answer is so simple and so powerful you will wonder why you never knew this before. *You get what you focus on.* The reason you get what you focus on is because *how you focus will lead to how you feel.* Your feelings are the surest indicator you have to measure what you are attracting. It is not possible to attract something you want when you are thinking about what you do not want. It is also not possible to attract what you want when you are feeling negative emotions. *The polarity of a negative emotion, or feeling, does not match up with a positive attraction.* I cannot attract a plane if I am feeling unhappy. I can only attract a plane when I am feeling positive emotions. *The polarity of a positive thought or emotion will attract a positive event.* When you feel good, you are moving toward what you want. Feeling good is a sure sign that the Law of Attraction is working in your favor.

I was happy to discover that it does not matter what I am feeling good about. Any good feeling will attract your desires. In other words, if I am attracting more money but my money situation stinks, I do not have to convince myself to feel good about money. I can choose to feel good about my beautiful wife or my three amazing daughters. I think about the friends I have or my last vacation; it does not matter! What matters is that I think about something that makes me happy until I feel happy. The moment I feel happy I am back in alignment with whatever I am in the process of manifesting.

For many years I tried lying to myself. If I was worrying about money, I would try to force myself to feel good about money. I learned the hard way that this only made me feel worse. A philosopher once said, "Any man can fly; all he need do is to sit under a tree for an hour without once thinking about flying." The more we try and *not* think about something, the more we will think about it. By the same token, if a money fear pops into my head and I try and sell myself on how great my money situation is, I will feel worse. If, however, I instead think about something positive that is totally unrelated to money, I will feel good. It does not matter what positive thing I shift to, it only matters that I focus on my replacement thought long enough to create a new emotion. I have a mental list of things that always make me feel good. Anytime I feel myself experiencing a negative emotion, I shift to one of the positive thoughts on my list. If you do not have a list of happy things, I strongly encourage you to compile one.

All of this "emotion shifting" goes well beyond the simple concept of positive thinking. Although I agree that positive thinking is a healthy attribute and can lead you to feeling better, I fear that many people may use positive thinking to mask a problem. Problems and challenges are indeed a part of life. When a challenge occurs, I strongly endorse hitting it head on!

One of the most successful entrepreneurs I know is a man named Bill Dallas. Bill is a legend in the mortgage industry and created an incredible life for himself. I enjoy watching Bill handle challenges. While others are running around like Chicken Little crying "The sky is falling! The sky is falling!" Bill is immediately looking for the opportunity that will emerge from the midst of all the chaos. He refers to problems as the "brutal facts." He encourages all of his employees to sit down and immediately confront the brutal facts. Notice, he does not pretend these facts do not exist or shift his thinking to something positive; this could be fatal in the mortgage industry. Once Bill and his team confront the brutal facts, a plan is immediately put in place to conquer the problem. With a strong plan in place that everyone believes will counter act the brutal facts, everyone begins to feel good again. Nobody on Bill's team spends anytime in denial. Running from the brutal facts or trying to convince yourself that the facts will change, will actually cause you to feel fear. I will say it again: fear is the enemy of positive attraction. Fear can only attract that which you are fearing. Once solutions are found to handle the brutal facts, Bill's team can shift their *focus* to the antidote, as opposed to the problem. Soon, the team becomes excited about the response to the challenge and no longer focuses on the challenge.

Please note the entire process I just referenced had nothing to do with positive or delusional thinking! We must confront whatever reality faces us at any given moment. We must also acknowledge that we either knowingly or unknowingly created our current reality using the Law of Attraction. If we created it, we must have had a reason. Also, if we created it, we can certainly change the reality using the very same law that brought it to us. Wow! Now we are talking about power, unlimited power to create anything we want. Can you see how we do not have to be positive thinkers to be happy and deliberate creators of our own destiny? Sometimes we have to deal with negative situations that arise. Confronting brutal facts is not positive or negative; it is simply the first step toward refocusing your thoughts and thus changing your emotions.

Here are the simple steps required to shift a problem to its antidote, or shift a negative emotion into a positive one:

1. You feel negative or low.

2. You search your thoughts until you find the one that feels bad.

3. You ask yourself, "What are the facts causing me to feel bad?"

4. You confront the facts one by one and respond to each one with a plan.

5. You begin to focus on each solution.

6. You begin to feel good about the solutions.

7. Your good feeling puts you back in alignment with your desires.

8. You are now attracting your original goal *and* the solutions to the problems you were feeling badly about!

What we did was transmute a problem that was creating a negative emotion (which, according to the Law of Attraction, was creating more problems), into a solution and a positive emotion. The positive emotion in turn was *guaranteed* to attract positive solutions in addition to the original desire you began attracting.

All of this happened under the irrefutable Law of Attraction. Remember, this is not magic or luck; it is a law of nature. Everything is made of energy and all energy has a vibration that will always seek out its vibrational match. You cannot feel good without attracting something good. Unfortunately, many of us go through life without specific intentions. So, although feeling good will certainly attract more reasons to feel good, we are, in a sense, wasting an additional opportunity since we are not focusing on a specific desire. For example, I am working on a new plane right now. When I feel good, I am fertilizing the seed of my new plane as well as just feeling good. Do not get me wrong—life is 100 percent about feeling good; but why not feel good *and* attract a beautiful new aircraft? Alternatively, I could *choose* to feel bad and magnetically attract more reasons to feel bad, all the while chasing my new airplane away from the hanger at the airport.

◆ ◆ ◆

At the beginning of chapter 4, I wrote, "You will know you have mastered the Law of Attraction when you become aware of all of your thoughts. Once aware of your thoughts, you can begin the vital process of shifting them toward your desires." Now you know that your thoughts are the first step toward your emotion. I will repeat the steps laid out earlier in this chapter:

1. A thought pops into your head.
2. You decide to focus on that thought.
3. Your emotion shifts according to the thought *you chose* to focus on!

Your emotions will attract their vibrational match!

Although there are numerous emotions we all experience, in *The Secret,* Esther Hicks said, "There are only two emotions from my perspective, good ones and bad ones." I agree with her, but should also point out that there are varying levels of feeling good or bad. I will list beginning with good and ending with bad—my personal opinion of the emotional scale. This list can and will vary for each of us. It really comes down to how we define each emotion. Here is my personal hierarchy of emotions:

Good Emotions

1. Blissful
2. Loved
3. Joyful
4. Peaceful
5. Happy
6. Prosperous
7. Accepted
8. Fulfilled
9. Safe
10. Serene

Bad Emotions

1. Fearful
2. Angry
3. Depressed
4. Jealous
5. Stressed
6. Guilty
7. Judged
8. Unworthy

9. Low

10. Confused

While listing these may seem unnecessary, I would argue that to shift an emotion we must first be able to identify it. Sometimes just feeling "bad" is not enough information to help change the situation. If I know that I am feeling bad because I am stressed, I can begin to identify and confront the cause of my stress. I can shift my focus to thoughts about how I can feel less stressed.

Often these hidden, or masked, thoughts and emotions can lead us to real breakthroughs. For example, if I identify my bad feelings as due to stress, I may realize I had overcommitted myself that day. Over commitment is a very uncomfortable feeling and the related stress will most likely attract more reasons to feel stressed—all of this without any conscious awareness on my part. Once I can identify the cause of feeling bad as stress through over commitment, I can immediately figure out how to start feeling better. For me, it is usually as simple as picking up the phone and postponing one meeting. I confront it, fix it, and immediately go back to feeling good and attracting what I want. If I ignore it, I keep feeling badly, rush around like a madman, drive my car like a crazy person, and no doubt attract a lot more problems than I started with.

Make your own list of emotions and keep it near you. When you feel bad, identify the bad feeling and cure it. If you don't, you quickly get out of alignment with your desires. Do not worry or beat yourself up when you experience negative emotions. There are two things to remember about them:

1. They are important messages about something you are masking; and the uncovering of the issue will lead you to feel really good!

2. A positive emotion is one hundred times more powerful than a negative one. This is a fact. Positive thoughts have been measured by scientists as one hundred times more powerful than negative ones. What this means is that you can use a negative emotion to help you uncover a problem, then immediately shift it to a positive emotion via the solution. Since the positive emotion is so much more powerful, you continue to attract your desires.

If you stay in a negative mode, you lose the benefit of positive attraction and you will begin to bring on the bad stuff. So, wake up! Your emotions are the key and they will keep you continually aware of whether you are in or out of alignment with your desires.

6

The Irrefutable Law of Focus

The Law of Focus is a simple and important component of the first two laws. The Law of Focus is intertwined with the Law of Emotion but still deserves its own chapter. Focus is everything! You get what you focus on! This cannot be said enough times and must be understood. In the last chapter we discussed how important it is to monitor your emotions and how your emotions can be used to determine if you are in or out of alignment with your desires.

The great thing about focus is how easy it is to control. By controlling your focus, you can head off any negative emotions. Once a negative emotion sets in, it can be challenging at times to shift away from the bad feeling. Although I laid out an effective strategy in chapter 5 for shifting a negative emotion into a positive one, the trick is that you have to want to make the shift. Let me explain. Feeling bad can create depression. Even light depression can cause apathy, which in turn dampens the desire to do anything that would make you feel better. This becomes a slippery slope! First I feel bad, and then I slip into an apathetic depression that keeps me from doing anything to feel better. While there are strategies to snap out this vicious circle, it would be beneficial to avoid the depression in the first place.

The feel-bad emotion is given life because you chose to focus on a thought that made you feel bad. The downhill feel-bad process begins with a single thought. As I previously mentioned, thoughts are difficult and perhaps impossible to control. Thousands of thoughts spring into our minds every day. Most of them go unnoticed and do not stay with you long enough to help or hurt you. For one reason or another, certain thoughts will take root in your mind and become the subject of your focus. The moment you catch yourself focusing on any given thought, stop yourself and take note if you are focusing on what you want or what you do not want. Either way, you will draw what you are focusing on into your life. When you can catch yourself focusing on what you do not want, you can easily shift your focus toward what you do want. The important thing is that you change your focus before you start dropping down the emotional scale and end up in fear or depression. Here is simple hierarchy to consider:

Event	**Ease of Control**	**Time to Shift**	**Conclusion**
Thought	Difficult or impossible	Come and go too fast to shift	Can't be controlled
Focus	Easy	Immediate	Easiest to control
Emotion	Difficult	Slow	Toughest to control

Would you agree, based on the above table, that *focus* is the place to focus? Where you apply your focus not only determines how you feel, it can greatly determine the overall quality of your life. I am amazed at how many people waste precious energy focusing on what they do not want instead of what they do want. Oftentimes, when asked to coach someone, I will begin by asking the person I am coaching what they want out of their life. Few of them actually tell me what they want because they get too wrapped up in telling me what they do not want. I often get answers such as, "I sure do not want to be in this dead-end job anymore." Or, "I just don't want to be in this terrible relationship any longer." Usually after listening for a few minutes to a long list of don't-wants, I will smile and again ask, "Okay, now that I have a pretty good idea of what you don't want, would you mind telling me what you *do* want?" Shockingly, I will typically be met with a blank stare and hear responses of people swearing they just *did* tell me what they want. Only after I play their exact words back to them do most people get the point. This exercise is a quick indicator for me to determine if I am working with a person who understands how to focus on what they want. It should come as no surprise that I am seldom asked to help someone who has already discovered where to place their focus. I am convinced that when someone reflexively answers by telling what they do want, I am talking with a person who most likely does not require my assistance.

By now, you most likely realize that the person who tells me what they do *not* want is stuck in a cycle of attracting what they do *not* want. The more they get of what they don't want, the more they focus on not wanting it. The more they focus on not wanting it, the more they get of it. And so it goes, over and over until something happens to break the cycle. The moment I can point this out and get someone to articulate what they *do* want, I can then change their focus. It is so simple when you become aware of the process! The more I do not want something, the more I get the thing I do not want. There is a saying that goes, "What you resist persists." Whoever said this clearly understood the Law of Attraction and the Law of Focus, and realized that focusing on resisting what you do not want will surely bring you more of what you do not want.

Let's imagine you have an annoying coworker; I will call him "Frank." Every morning when you wake up, you think about how much you dislike Frank. In fact, without even realizing it you have become obsessed with your dislike of him. Frank certainly deserves to be disliked; he is a know-it-all and is constantly getting everyone around him in trouble. The worst part about Frank is that he is lazy and always takes credit for everything everyone else does. The boss does not seem to realize this and in fact is always complimenting Frank for work he did not do. Because the boss is blind to what is going on, Frank keeps getting paid more and more money, has his own parking space, and most likely will get the next promotion. You hate Frank! You hate him so much that it would be difficult for me to get you to find anything positive about him. Hence is the rub: the more you resist Frank and focus on your dislike of him, the more you draw him nearer to you. We are again dealing with the irrefutable Law of Attraction, which your focus has now invoked!

I have been down this road not only myself but also with many people I mentor. The moment I start explaining to someone that their dislike of Frank is creating more of Frank, they start trying to justify their feelings. They have become so invested in their negative feelings for Frank that they cannot see their way out of them. Have you ever found yourself in a situation like this? Your negative focus can become an addiction; the more you focus on this negative thing, the more you need to focus on it. All the while, Frank has become so powerful that he owns you. You have given all of your power to Frank! The Law of Attraction will grow stronger and you will continue to find yourself wherever Frank is.

If you are smart and evolved, you will quickly deploy the Law of Focus and almost immediately shift the situation. The only other legal and moral answer would be to quit your job. The universe has a funny way of dealing with us when we try to skirt any of the irrefutable laws. I can almost guarantee you that when you find a new job, there will be a brand-new Frank just waiting for you. Why? Because by quitting, all you have done is to treat the symptom. The illness that needed treating was your failure to use and master the Law of Focus. It is so simple; I smile as I type this information!

Hopefully, we have ruled out running from the problem, thus leaving us to discuss some easy ways to shift our focus away from Frank and treat the root cause of your focus on your dislike of him. There are two ways to shift your focus away from hating Frank. The first is finding a way to forgive or love Frank; the second is to stop focusing on Frank altogether.

Many people may find the first way difficult to employ, as it involves a very forgiving and loving approach. Sadly, it is difficult for many of us to forgive or to love Frank. If you have spent months hating somebody, are you the type of person who can suddenly find good and saintly qualities in that person?

I have a situation I am dealing with in my business and I can emphatically tell you, it is tough to see the good when you are constantly frustrated at someone. I will tell you, if you can use this method and love someone who may be wronging you; it is *very* liberating and effective. The peace that can come from loving your enemy is indescribable. I have practiced this now for many years and I am finally able to succeed some of the time. Imagine if you could wake up one morning and suddenly feel compassion for Frank? What if you learned he was an abused or abandoned child, would this help you to love him? How about if one day you got in a terrible jam and Frank was the first to come to your rescue? Are you getting the picture yet?

The course in miracles teaches us that Frank's behavior is a cry for love. Nobody ever taught Frank how to ask for or receive love. Instead Frank is motivated by his fear of not being loved. I will tell you again, fear is the most powerful attractor I know. Frank's fear of not being loved keeps attracting to him people like you, who hate him. Poor Frank has *no* idea of the unloving patterns he continues to create in his life. And you continue to play into the drama as if you have been cast in a play that Frank directs. Talk about giving away your power! If you can just convince yourself of these facts, you may be able to begin feeling compassion for Frank and you may begin realizing how matched up your two polarities have become. The moment you begin to feel love and compassion for poor Frank, you shift the energy, change your polarity, and the attraction stops. I mean, it literally stops! The Law of Attraction will not allow you to even be in the same room with Frank. You cannot nor will you ever change Frank; it is not your job or responsibility. Your job is to either stop focusing on Frank or start focusing on what is good about Frank. Either way you choose is great. Both choices will change your focus away from what you hate about Frank, thus changing the vibration and ending the attraction of Frank.

As I stated earlier, some of you will struggle with the concept of loving a person you hate. Although I hope you will try this method because it is the healthier and more effective one, I will provide you with a back-up strategy. Simply, forget Frank! Each time Frank creeps into your mind, you must shift your focus toward something that makes you happy. By the way, the thought cannot have anything to do with Frank, such as having him kidnapped or disappear. You have to focus to a totally non-Frank-related subject and it needs to be a subject that pleases you. Earlier in the book, I mentioned keeping a list of things that make you happy. You can think about your wife, your child, your favorite pet, your first girlfriend, your goldfish, your car, a walk on the beach, a date you had last night, the beautiful fall weather, your next vacation, your last vacation, or winning the lottery. It doesn't matter, as long as it causes you to feel joy and you are able think about it long enough to forget Frank.

Twenty years ago I was sued by a nasty old man. The lawsuit cost me a small fortune and occupied countless hours of my spare time. At that time, I read a book by Emmet Fox. The book was full of parables and stories that helped me find peace at that time in my life. Twenty years later, I cannot remember the title of the book but I remember two stories that helped me shift my focus. I can honestly tell you that within weeks of shifting my focus away from the man who was suing me, the lawsuit quietly and effortlessly disappeared. Really, it did! One day, I was vigorously defending myself and the next day, for no known or apparent reason, the lawsuit was dropped.

First, I read a short parable that Mr. Fox wrote, called "Bear Hugs Kettle." I will paraphrase the story because I no longer have the book. One day a giant grizzly bear walked up to a campsite. Fortunately, there were no people around, but there was a red-hot campfire with a kettle full of delicious food brewing. The bear was hungry and could smell the hot food. He immediately walked up to campfire and while standing on his two rear legs, picked up the red-hot kettle. Naturally, the bear was instantly burned and became angry. When bears become angry, their reflex is to hug tighter. As the bear hugged the kettle more tightly, he was burned even more severely, which in turn caused him to hug the kettle even more tightly. The bear continued to hug the kettle until he perished.

This story turned on a light bulb in my mind. The lawsuit brought on by the nasty old man was my kettle and the angrier I became about the lawsuit, the more tightly I hugged the kettle. I knew I needed to let go of the kettle before it burned me to death, but I really did not know how to let go. It seems I was operating under the same *false* survival instinct as the bear.

Fortunately, I then read another parable in the same book, which provided me with a strategy to let go of the kettle. Emmet Fox called this one, "The Golden Key." Once again, I will need to paraphrase the concept behind the story. I will tell you that I have used this concept to shift my focus and drop the kettle thousands of times over the last twenty years. The idea is to take whatever is bothering you—let's say it's Frank again—and then to form a strong picture of it (Frank) in your mind. For a moment this will sound counterintuitive to everything I have been teaching you, but stay with me. Once you have formed the picture of Frank, or whatever it is your are pushing against, immediately picture a giant golden key. In your mind's eye, use the golden key to push the picture of Frank firmly out of your head. Right behind the golden key, a new picture must follow. The new picture should be something you absolutely adore. I am talking about something that is so special to you that you cannot help immediately smiling and feeling warm all over. For me at that time, it was my four-year-old daughter. Forgive me for bragging, but she had the cutest and sweetest face I had ever seen in my entire life. Every time I looked at Ashley, I had to smile and I was (and still am) completely obsessed with her! She made me laugh, she made me proud, and she gave me purpose. You need to find your "Ashley" for this exercise. The main point to this exercise is that we first picture what we do not want; we then, using the golden key, replace the picture with something we adore. The new picture does not have to be a person, it can be anything that makes you feel good, including someplace you have been or long to go.

Let's quickly review this chapter:

1. You get what you focus on.

2. Be sure to focus on what you want.

3. Focus is easier to control than your thoughts or your emotions.

4. "What you resist will persist."

5. Don't hug the kettle.

6. You can "golden-key away" your problems and thus change your focus.

7

The Irrefutable Law of Gratitude

As a preface to this chapter, let's do a simple exercise together. What I would like you to do is to think for a moment about something you are grateful for. Perhaps you are grateful for a loved one in your life. You may also be grateful for your car, your job, the place you live, your physical body, or anything else. All I ask is that you pick something you are truly grateful about. Okay, have you chosen something you are grateful about? Now, go deeper into the thought and feeling of gratitude. Think about how much better your life is for having this person or thing in it. Think about the benefits that this person or thing bring you on a daily basis. See yourself being with the object of your gratitude. Are you there? Are you warmly wrapped within a cocoon of gratitude? How does it feel? Pretty good, I'll bet! Okay, what is my point? My point is that it is impossible to feel truly grateful and bad at the same moment. Totally and 100 percent impossible!

I make this point because the name of the game is feeling good. You cannot feel good and attract something bad at the same time. On the other hand, you cannot feel bad and attract prosperity in the same moment. You have to feel good feelings to attract good stuff! So, if feeling grateful makes you feel good, it would seem to me to be a worthwhile emotion to cultivate.

You could argue, "Why spend a chapter on gratitude? If the end game is feeling good, why not write a chapter on swimming with dolphins, or holding a baby, or being with your best friend?" The reason to focus on gratitude is that gratitude has *extra* magnetic powers of attraction. Gratitude is the opposite of fear and has even greater magnetic powers than fear. We must learn to focus on things that will attract heavy doses of our desires to us. Gratitude is the best way I have learned to say "thank you" to the universe and at the same time say, *"More, please!"* The more we feel grateful for something the faster it will multiply.

First, let's look at this from a relationship point of view. If you have a happy and fulfilling relationship, I am willing to wager that you are in constant appreciation of the person you are in relationship with. I find the more I express gratitude toward my wife, the more she seems to want to support me. It makes sense, both spiritually and practically. From a practical standpoint, most of us want to be appreciated. So, the more we feel appreciated, the more we want to do to continue the feeling of appreciation. From a spiritual standpoint, whatever we give our attention to, will grow. When I am appreciating and feeling grateful toward my wife, I am focusing positive energy toward her, which will in turn attract more reasons for me to appreciate her.

Also, gratitude is the antidote of fear. You cannot feel fearful and grateful at the same time. Gratitude will attract prosperity toward you and fear will repel it. For this reason, it is important to get in a daily habit of being grateful. I begin every morning going through an entire list of everything I am grateful toward. I find it is best to run through this list first thing in the morning and preferably while taking a nice, brisk walk in the clear morning air. I will share my list and the process I use with you, in hopes that it will stimulate the creation of your own list:

Thank you, God, for all of the amazing blessings that I have and thank you for granting me the power to continue to create anything my heart desires. I am grateful and thankful for:

- *This beautiful morning*
- *My incredible health*
- *The best wife in the entire world*
- *My three amazing daughters [I mention their names] and the great times we have together and the love I feel on a daily basis from them*
- *All the great friends that I have [I mention every one of their names]*
- *All of my coworkers [I mention the names of the ones I regularly interface with] and how vital each one of them is to my success and happiness*
- *My four dogs, Guido, Vinnie, Otis, and Prince, and all the laughs and love they provide me*
- *My cat, Snowballs*
- *My horse, Blue*
- *My family's dream house in the country [I even describe everything I love about my house]*
- *Our home in Mexico*
- *My dream airplane and the freedom it provides me*
- *My beautiful and fun BMW and the good feelings I get from driving it*
- *My wife's beautiful car and how good and safe it makes her feel*
- *Each of my daughter's cars and the ability to purchase them new cars*

- *My motorcycles and the freedom from traffic they provide me*
- *Our motor coach and the great times we spend together traveling as a family in it*
- *My off-road vehicles and the exhilaration that comes from each one of them*
- *My golf cart and how much fun my youngest daughter and I have cruising around the neighborhood in it*
- *My country club membership and all the friends I get to take golfing*
- *My job*
- *My company*
- *My Mexico construction project*
- *My speaking and coaching career*
- *My incredible, self-manifested, made-to-order life!*

It takes me a long-time to go through my list because I spend a lot of time thinking about and feeling grateful for every item on the list.

This is an important point! You should not simply read your list without feeling. You would be missing the point of the exercise. The point is to create and submerge yourself in the feeling of gratitude. You may have noticed that my list contains a lot of things to be grateful for. I can assure you it was not always that way! I can also assure you that the list grew for one primary reason ... *because I focused on it*. In fact, I focused everyday *with passion* on my list of things to be grateful for. What happens when we focus on something? By now you had better have said, "We attract it!" Gratitude is fun! Not only do I get what I am focusing on, I also get a multiplier effect by focusing on what I am grateful for. My list keeps growing and at times I cannot believe it myself. Everyday when I go through the list, I get so excited and happy that I have to pinch myself. How can starting your morning feeling like that not be a good thing?

Last year I started a new venture and it was starting off pretty slowly. I also was quickly learning that I did not really enjoy my new business. To make matters worse, I plowed several hundred thousand dollars into the company. Well, all this slowly allowed fear to creep in and I knew that if I focused on the fears, I would surely fail. Luckily I shared those feelings of fear with Karen Vice, my Anthony Robbins—assigned coach. Thankfully, Karen reminded me that gratitude is the antidote for fear and asked me to perform an exercise. I laughed and said, "Are you crazy? Are you actually telling me, the most grateful guy on the planet, to practice gratitude? Ha!" I said. I went on to inform Karen of my daily gratitude ritual and suggested we focus on something different.

She persisted and reminded me that gratitude is the enemy and destroyer of fear and if I was feeling fearful, I needed to practice even more gratitude. With that, she asked me to make a list of two hundred things I felt grateful for and once the list was completed, I was to transfer each item onto a 3"x5" card. Two hundred items of gratitude is a lot to think about and the list took a fair amount of time to complete. It was also monotonous filling out the two hundred cards, each with one item of gratitude. I was then told to randomly pull three cards every day and to spend that day focusing extensively on the three cards. I put each card in my planner and repeatedly read each card, sometimes twenty times per day. It worked. Within a couple of weeks, before a fearful thought could even find its way into my mind, it became instantly replaced with a grateful thought. Wow, talk about spontaneous transmutation of a negative emotion into a positive one! Karen was right! Even though, I, the "master of gratitude," had been practicing feeling grateful every morning, it still was not enough at that time in my life.

How will you deploy your "attitude of gratitude"? I highly recommend you begin by making a *long* list of every possible thing you have to be grateful for. My coach Karen Vice told me about one of her clients who had been homeless at one point in her life. Her list really hit home for me and made me realize just how grateful I was. The women had things on her list like clean water to drink, a toothbrush, warm water, clean clothes, a pillow, sheets, a roof over her head, food from the grocery store (as opposed to the streets), and eating utensils. I could go on, but I suppose you understand my point. Even the most unfortunate of you who have found your way to this book; most likely have a list of things you can feel grateful for. You should even be grateful for the air you breathe and the sun that warms your face. If you start with anything you have to be thankful for, before you know it, your list will grow to include the greatest of your heart's desires.

The challenge is that most of us push away things we are not grateful for and somehow hope things will get better. For example, perhaps you have an old car and you feel ashamed of it. You feel no joy from this car and do not take care of it. The car is probably filthy dirty and has not had an oil change for many thousands of miles. All you ever do is complain about how much your hate your ugly car. Have you ever felt this way about anything you owned? If you did, you probably were not aware of how ungrateful you were behaving. If being grateful attracts more of what you are grateful for, I can assure you being ungrateful will attract more of what you are ungrateful for. Once again, we are discussing the Law of Attraction and how it dances with the Law of Gratitude. Hating your old car is the surest way I know of to remain stuck with your old car. Hating your car will also cause bad things to happen to it. The car you hate is more likely to break down, get towed, and cause accidents. The only bad thing that will not happen to the car you hate, is that it will *not* get stolen, for theft would free you from your nasty car and you cannot be freed from that which you push against. The more you hate the car, the more the Laws of Attraction and Gratitude will draw situations and events that will help you to continue hating the car.

For contrast, let's try the opposite approach. What do you think would happen if you could find a way to love and *appreciate* the car you have hated? What would happen if you washed and waxed her everyday? How about rotating the tires, changing the oil, and replacing the spark plugs? Imagine waking up in the morning and giving thanks for the car that you do have. You could try appreciating the fact that you do not have to ride the bus or walk to work. Feeling grateful for the car you do have will cause you to take better care of it and eventually your good feeling will attract the events and circumstances necessary to get yourself a new car. What you put your attention to will grow; feeling grateful is the best way to thank the universe and ask for, "More please?"

Have you ever begun thinking about a new car and then immediately started thinking about all the things you did not like about your old car? I suppose people do this to help themselves justify the purchase of the new car. When I was younger, it seemed each time I wanted a new car, things would start going wrong with my old car—bad things, like blown head gaskets or cylinders. Now that I understand the Law of Gratitude I understand why this kept happening to me. The moment I decided on a new car, I would begin focusing on what I hated about my old car. The attraction would immediately kick in and start attracting some real reasons for me to hate my car. The more I focused on the hate for my old car, the worse it became. I can remember times when that old car would get so bad that I could not even sell it; I literally became magnetized to the car I hated!

Now when I decide on a new car, I am careful to continue to appreciate my old car. I never pull my love or appreciation out of the old car. It is not necessary to justify the new car by bashing the old car; it is much more effective to love the old car and use that gratitude to attract a beautiful new one. The same is true with anything. If you long for a big new house, the best thing you can do is begin by appreciating and being grateful for your little old house. The gratitude you feel for your old house will put you on a fast track toward your new home.

Let's review the Law of Gratitude:

1. Being grateful will magnetize what you want faster.
2. Gratitude is a way of saying "thank you" to the universe.
3. Gratitude also says, "More please" to the universe.
4. Gratitude is the antidote to fear.
5. You cannot feel fearful and grateful at the same time.
6. Feeling grateful makes you feel good.
7. Feeling grateful will help you replace the things you no longer want with the new things you do want.

8

The Irrefutable Law of intention

Intention is the seed of attraction. Stating your intention is the mandatory first step toward attracting your desires. You can state your intentions verbally or in writing; I suggest both. A written intention is similar to writing out an abbreviated goal. It should be clear, concise and leave no room for questions. Here are a few examples of properly written intentions:

- I intend to have a new home within one year.
- I intend to have a higher paying job within six months.
- I will attract a loving relationship in the next six months.

The universe is both literal and specific. This is important to keep in mind anytime you plant your seed of intention into the fertile grounds of attraction. Whatever you intend to have through your intention statement will come to you, provided you give the intended desire the focus it needs. An intention should always be stated in the affirmative. You should always avoid statements like:

- I intend to *stop* drinking.
- I will *lose* weight.

- I will *stop* being in debt.
- I will *get out* of my low-paying job.

Can you see that all of these statements are negative? They each contain something not wanted as opposed to something desired. I would restate each the above statements as follows:

- I intend to be happy and sober.
- I intend to have a thirty-two-inch waist and 10 percent body fat by year's end.
- I will have an abundance of excess income within six months.
- I intend to attract a fantastic and high-paying job.

While the restatement may seem to have only subtle differences, the universe and Law of Attraction will view them as *completely* different. The first set of intentions will cause your focus to be upon what you do *not* want. The second set of intentions focus on what you *do* want. If we are to consider intentions as seeds, we should be sure we do not plant an onion in the cornfield!

I have heard several people say that you should state an intention as if it has already happened. In other words, you could write your intentions like this:

- I have attracted a new car.
- I am thankful for my new house.
- I am grateful for the new job I have attracted.

There is good logic in stating intentions this way, because the universe cannot distinguish the present from the future. If you state something as if it has already happened, it is a wake-up call to the Law of Attraction. However, I have found this to be difficult and do not recommend it. When my conscious mind hears me stating a lie, it resists the intention and makes it harder for me to focus on its achievement.

I have also found it effective to state my intention as it relates to the process of attraction. Here are a few examples:

- I am so happy now that I am attracting a new car.
- I love the idea that I am attracting a new house.
- I so proud to be attracting a great new job.

All of these statements are both positive and believable to your conscious mind. In all cases, your intentions must be clear, concise, and specific. You should leave no room for interpretation. If you leave the Law of Attraction and the universe to guess, you may not always like what comes to you. Remember, the intention statement is the first step toward activating the vibrational energy match required to manifest your desire.

Intentions can also be thought of as affirmations. I can tell you firsthand that affirmations *do* work very effectively. I have learned how to transmute almost any fear or thought through consistent affirmations. For instance, it has been years since I have had a cold or the flu. I have not had a fever and I do not stay home sick from work. I laugh to myself when I hear people comment on it being cold or flu season. The reason I find this amusing is that the people who tell you this are the very people who get sick every flu season. These are the same folks who say, "Get away from me, I don't want to catch your cold." They will also tell you how many germs are on airplanes and how every year when their kid starts school, they bring home germs and make the whole house sick. I became convinced many years ago, that if germs made people sick, then everyone on the planet would always be sick.

I began wondering why some people at work got sick, while others did not. I mean, both people were around the same person sneezing all day and yet only one of them "caught the germ." The answer became obvious to me due to my knowledge of the Law of Attraction. Everything in the universe is energy, right? If everything is made up of energy and all energy has a unique vibration, then of course a cold germ also is made up of vibrational energy. The cold germ will look for its vibrational match, just like anything else will. If this is all true, and I have proven to myself many times that it is true, then the cold germ will find the person who is focusing on getting sick.

Knowing this is helpful but I have also found a way to practice this truth. Every time I get around someone who is sick, coughing, or sneezing, I affirm to myself the following, "I am healthy and strong." I will repeat this affirmation until I completely forget about the sick person in the room. If they sneeze again and remind me of their presence, I will repeat the affirmation again and again and again. Sometimes, I feel a slight twinge of a sore throat or a tickle in my throat, and I then immediately begin stating the "I am healthy and strong"affirmation. You will *never* hear me say; "Uh-oh, I think I'm getting sick" I will not stop repeating the affirmation until I have forgotten about what was bothering me in the first place.

Affirmations can become habitual if you practice them enough. Coming up with and habitually repeating a positive affirmation is a great thing to do. Remember, an affirmation is the same as an intention statement. Stating your intention is like planting the seed of your desire into the soil of attraction. Each time you repeat your intention, you are placing your focus upon it and thus you are attracting what you are focusing on.

Each morning on my way to work, I state the following affirmation, "I am healthy, wealthy, and happy." I also mix up the affirmation with an intention statement. When stating the words as an intention, I say, "I attract health, wealth, and happiness." Can you imagine how happy I feel by the time I arrive at the office?

The first thirty minutes after I wake up are dedicated to gratitude. As I stated in the last chapter, I passionately run through my entire list of things I am grateful for having. Then, I get on my motorcycle or in my car and I start repeating, "I attract health, wealth, and happiness." You can't say this a few hundred times without feeling pretty damn healthy, wealthy, and happy. These affirmations repeated after thirty minutes of feeling grateful keep me fully aligned with my desires.

You may be thinking, "Who the heck wants to waste all that time in their car chanting some goofy affirmations?" If so, I would challenge you to ask yourself what you do in the car. I often see people either looking stressed or completely expressionless while driving. Especially in Los Angeles, where we shoot each other on the freeways! I firmly believe if you are not controlling your thoughts, they are controlling you. My point is that every free moment is a gift that can be used for deliberate creation. When driving in your car, you can be focusing on what you intend to create in your life. The alternative is that your mind wanders into "no man's land," a land where we become completely unaware of our thoughts or focus. A land where we also unconsciously create things we do not want. If you only get one thing out of this entire book, I hope it will be a new awareness that you are always creating something. Many people unconsciously create what they do not want in life, while the masters of life consciously create in every waking moment. Please wake up and create using deliberate intent. Free yourself from the constraints of "no man's land," where you just keep getting what you what do not want and never realize why you got it.

Driving your car is a likely place to slip away into the land of unconscious creation. I am extra careful with my thoughts while driving. Again I ask you, what do you do in your car? I hope you will try using the time to state your intentions and begin the magical attraction process.

Earlier I compared an intention statement to the planting of a seed into the fertile soil of the Law of Attraction. This is both a true and excellent comparison for you to use as a reference. I also like to think about my intention statement as broadcasting out a radio signal into the universe, so that the Law of Attraction can pick up the frequency. I have read almost every book Deepak Chopra has written and in his book, *The Seven Spiritual Habits of Success,* Chopra writes about the Law of Intention as one of his seven laws. In his explanation, Chopra makes an important point: any intention should be cast from a calm mind. If your mind is turbulent and full of fear or doubt, your message will not be heard over your own static. A calm and confident mind has the ability to broadcast a clear signal that can be received from an infinite audience. Chopra compared casting an intention to casting a stone into a calm lake; even the smallest stone will ripple for miles. Alternatively he compared casting a large building into the rough ocean; the ripples will not be felt. Whether you choose to think of broadcasting your message as a radio signal without static or as a stone hitting calm waters, it does not matter. All that matters is that when you do cast your intention out to the universe, you do it with a calm, clear, and confident mind.

Lastly, and back to the seed comparison, when you plant the seed of your intention, leave it alone and let it grow. I have heard many authors state this and yet I have still caught myself doing the opposite over the years. Many of us plant the seed and then we focus all of our energy on wondering if the seed will grow. It will grow, unless you dig it up to see if it is growing. Seems obvious, right? You would never really dig up a seed in your garden to check if it is growing. Yet, when we plant our intentions, many of us have a tendency to dig them up. We dig our intentions out of the ground when we do any of the following:

- Doubt that they will grow
- Fear that they will not grow
- Wonder how they will grow
- Wonder if we deserve them to grow

By the law of nature, your intentions must grow if you do not dig them up! It would be helpful if you water and fertilize the seeds of your intentions. Here are the ways that I accomplish this task:

- Practice daily gratitude
- Visualize the obtainment of my desires
- Visualize other times in my life when my intentions have come to me
- Meditate
- Stay happy and in alignment with my intentions
- Help others get what they want
- Use affirmations
- Write down and read my intentions daily

We are the lucky species because we posses a central nervous system that allows us to think, process, and react. That's the good news! The bad news is that we must remember to use our systems for creating.

The truth is that everything in the universe has intelligence, including every single cell in your body. We know this because everything in the universe is made of vibrational energy. Each subatomic particle has the intelligence to be wherever it is supposed to be at any given second. If everything is made up of exactly the same stuff—again I will remind you that the inside of an acorn looks identical to the inside of the seed of a rose bush under a powerful enough microscope—then how does an acorn become an oak tree and a rose seed become a rose bush? Two reasons, the first being intention and the second being intelligence. The energy and subatomic particles of an acorn contain the intention and intelligence to become an oak tree, just as the energy of a rose seed contains the intention and intelligence to become a rose bush.

We are the same with one exception. We have a central nervous system that requires us to state our intention. This is good news and leads us to free will! Through our intentions, we have the free will to do or become *anything* we desire. The acorn contains the energy with the predestined intention to become an oak tree.

I suggest you use your intentions and your free will and start attracting the life you want to have right now! Let's review the Law of Intention:

1. Intention is the seed of manifestation.
2. Intentions should be clear, concise, and specific.
3. Intentions should always be stated in a positive manner.
4. Intentions should be repeated daily.
5. Intentions are also considered affirmations and affirmations can be used to transmute fear and doubt.
6. We should not dig up the seeds of our intentions.
7. We should water and fertilize our intentions daily.
8. Everything in the universe grows because of intention.

9

The Irrefutable Law of Least Effort

The Law of Least Effort is my favorite law. My wife and I also refer to this law as the "law of opposites." Some of you will think I am crazy and in fact may even be offended by my interpretation of this law. The reason you could be offended is because this law goes against many things that most of us have been taught and, frankly, it just seems too easy.

In the first chapter of this book, I mentioned some of the accidental programming I received from my father. One of my dad's false beliefs was that "Nothing good comes easy." I can still remember those exact words ringing through my ears as a child. I must again say my dad was not at all attempting to be negative or to handicap my belief system. He truly believed his words and personal paradigms would prepare me for the "real world." My dad taught what he believed to be true and he got his beliefs from my grandfather. As I said before, my grandpa was one of the greatest men to ever walk the earth.

Allow me to list a few statements that we have all heard, that have led us to believe life is a struggle:

- Nothing good comes easy (my dad's favorite)
- If it were easy, everyone would be doing it

- Big money, big stress (this one I used in my younger days)
- You have to pay your dues (another one of my dad's)
- Life is hard and then we die
- Life is full of challenges
- What does not kill us, makes us stronger

Although there may be some truth to some of these statements, I now interpret them entirely differently from the way I used to.

For instance, I agree that life can have challenges, although I no longer equate "challenge" with "struggle." By using the laws I have shared with you, you will quickly come to believe that *you* are creator of both your challenges and your solutions. When you empower yourself with the belief that you and you alone brought a challenge into your life by using the Law of Attraction, it is easy to then attract the solution. Napoleon Hill, in *Think and Grow Rich*, said over fifty years ago, "Every failure contains within it a seed of equal or greater opportunity." Mr. Hill was right! If you have the power to attract a failure, you certainly have to power to attract an opportunity much greater than the failure. I believe the same to be true for problems and challenges.

At a glance, each of the statements I listed above contains a negative message. We have all grown up hearing the same messages and we have all been taught to believe that life is not easy. I can now tell you ... *we were deceived!* Life does not have to be a struggle; it can flow from one beautiful day to the next. Over the past several years, I have had the benefit of watching many people become wealthy people. They did not struggle prior to obtaining wealth and they certainly do not struggle now. I will admit that many of them worked long hours and applied a great deal of energy toward their wealth, but it was not a struggle. Never confuse time and energy spent on a project with struggling. This book has required many late nights and countless hours, but I promise you, I have not struggled one bit with the process. In fact, every time I have a minute to sit down and write, I get excited! Please don't think I am crazy, but I actually get goose bumps when I think about writing this book. Does that sound like a struggle?

Struggling comes from doing things that you dislike. I don't recommend spending time doing anything you dislike. This may sound like an extreme or fallacious thing to say, but I mean it. A couple of years ago, I worked for one of the largest companies in the world. They paid me over a million dollars per year to run their national sales force and I quit! I quit without having any idea what I would do next and I quit without knowing if anyone would ever pay me that much again. I quit because I stopped having fun! The job became a struggle and I know that when I struggle, I am not in alignment with my desires. When struggling, I am working against the Law of Attraction instead of allowing it to work for me.

In the beginning the job was fun. It was the most fun I'd ever had and I was honored to work with some of the greatest people in the industry. Everyday we laughed, collaborated, and created. We had so much fun and got along so well as a management team that the company grew from three hundred people to three thousand people in less than three years. The company went from funding four hundred million dollars per month in mortgages to three billion dollars per month in mortgages. See what happens when you love what you are doing? Two years later, the company is still about the same size and may have even shrunk somewhat. Not because I left; I was quite replaceable. The company stopped growing because everyone started struggling. I simply had the courage to walk away.

Let me describe an average day for one of the wealthiest men I know. He lives in Portugal in an amazing home overlooking the sea. He most likely will not like to be named, so I will call him "Joe." He wakes up each day when his eyes open. I am not trying to be funny, I am making a point that most of us wake up to something. Some wake up to an alarm clock, a noise in the kitchen, or some other external event. Joe wakes when his eyes open, meaning the moment he desires to awaken. His eyes normally open around 9:30 a.m.; he looks to right of his satin pillow, removes his ear plugs and eye mask and finds a silver tray with piping hot coffee and an amazing assortment of fruit and breads. I promise you I am not making this story up!

After finishing some fruit and drinking some coffee, Joe slowly gets up and wanders into his study, which has an obstructed view of the Lisbon Sea. He checks his stocks and glances at his calendar to see when his first appointment is, knowing it will not be before 2:00 p.m. Joe never schedules anything before lunch. He then takes a long walk along the beach, and begins making phone calls while walking in the sand. He walks very slowly and speaks deliberately. Nothing about Joe is hasty or rushed; he believes rushing is too stressful and stress ruins his day. He normally finishes his walk at the same time he finishes his phone calls. When he gets back into his home, one of his daughters is almost always there with his grandchildren. He plays with the grandkids and then goes into his bedroom and begins getting ready for the rest of his day.

Joe's day continues pretty much the same way until evening. He spends most evenings at the backgammon club, laughing, joking, and playing with some of the top-ranked backgammon players in the world. Dinner with family and friends never starts before ten at night and he never eats alone. Joe is a very social man.

Many years ago, I spent a month with Joe in Portugal and I jokingly said, "Man, it must be nice to have your life." He looked at me like I was crazy and said, "Anyone can have my life, it was not reserved solely for me." I said, "Yes, but being a billionaire certainly helps." He stared at me and then said, *"My money did not create my life style, my life style created my money."* Wow! I'm not sure if Joe consciously practices the six laws I have written about, but I do know at some level he understands them quite well. Joe explained to me that he has always enjoyed everything he does. Essentially, if it were not fun, Joe did not do it. Living this happy life continually engaged the Law of Attraction, which continued to deliver him more good times.

Okay, now let me uncover the specifics of the Law of Least Effort. When we follow the Six Irrefutable Laws of Prosperity, we will automatically end up exactly where we need to be. If we continually end up exactly where we need to be, why would we struggle? We struggle when we are not where we need or want to be. We struggle out of jobs and out of relationships. We struggle away from cars and people we do not like. The laws I have articulated will *not* allow you to end up anywhere you do not want to be. Life is hard for people who unconsciously create what they do not want. Life is hard for people who spend their energy focusing on what they do *not* want. Life is hard for people who are ungrateful and unhappy. As you now know, I will get what I focus on. If I focus on what I do not want, I will invoke the Law of Attraction, wake up millions of subatomic particles, and begin the process of attracting exactly what I do not want. Once I get what I do not want, now I have to struggle away from it. The Law of Attraction will keep me bound to whatever I am struggling against. It has to; the more I focus on getting away from something, the more energy I attract toward the thing I am attempting to escape from. That is what I call a struggle!

Struggle also comes from trying to force things to happen. Have you ever tried to force magnets with reverse polarity together? You can't do it! They run from one another; the polarity of each magnet will not allow the two magnets to stay together no matter how hard you try to force them. Life and the Law of Attraction work the same way. Forcing is the same as struggling. When I want something to happen, I focus on it. I keep focusing on it until I get it. Let's say I want a new car and I begin to focus on one. Do I wake up one day and magically find one in my garage? Probably not, although that would be cool! What happens is that my intense focus and visualization followed by a clear intention statement will wake up the Law of Attraction. The Law of Attraction will begin to seek out circumstances and events necessary for me to get a new car. My job is not to try and figure out how I will get my new car. My simple job is to pay attention and follow the clues that Law of Attraction will lay in front of me. Struggling or second guessing the Law of Attraction will only make it more difficult to find the clues.

What you need you to know is that there are infinite possibilities swirling around you at every given second. You cannot see all of this energy swirling, but you can't see radio or television waves, either. Our inability to see something does not mean it does not exist! At first, all this vibrational activity swirling around me does not mean much. Each swirling subatomic particle is simply a possibility of what could become. When I state my intention and increase my focus, I shift the millions of possibilities into probabilities. Here is a list of things that could happen when I begin focusing on my new car:

- Someone I know could randomly offer to buy my old car.
- My fully insured old car could be stolen.
- I could get a pay raise.
- I could be offered a promotion or new job.
- Someone could book me on a speaking tour.
- Twenty new people could hire me as their coach.
- BMW could recall my old car and offer me a new one.
- I could win the lottery (I guess I should buy a ticket).

- I could win a school raffle.

The list of possibilities could be as long as this entire book. I think you would agree that any of these events could be possible. The point is, we simply do not know, nor should we care, how the car will come to us. We simply need to practice the six laws of prosperity. Struggle will only come into play if I start focusing on *not* wanting my old car.

In 1998 I was the CEO of a public company. I told the story of how I attracted this job earlier in this book. Although I had attracted my dream job, I had also bit off more than I could chew at the time. Needless to say, I caused myself to struggle, trying to turn around the unhealthy and capital-starved company. I was constantly on airplanes, flying back and forth to New York. I missed my family and I was tired beyond belief. Without realizing it, I had put myself on a treadmill and I had begun attracting a lot of things I did not want. In fact, my wife often heard me say, "I don't want to go back to New York and meet with another arrogant fund manager." Or, "I don't want to fly all the way to New York and have dinner with a nasty old stock analyst". At that time, I was desperately trying to get my company on Wall Street's radar screen. We had a solid business model but needed to attract capital and analyst coverage so the major brokerage houses would buy our stock.

One day, as I was literally throwing clothes into a suitcase, my wife came into the bedroom and said, "You're going again?" I could tell she wasn't happy to see me leaving on yet another long trip. My wife has never been possessive or jealous; she simply was missing me and did not like seeing me unhappy. Missing me and wanting me to be happy gave her the motivation to start asking some questions. She asked whom I was meeting and why I was meeting them. Again, this was not being nosey or possessive; it was time for her to understand these trips, which were torturing me. The answers I provided led to more questions. She wanted to know things like.

Do you like the guy you're going to meet?
Do you think he can help you?
Is there someone you would rather be meeting?
What would happen if you did not take the trip?
Then appeared the killer question....
What do you want to have happen as a result of these meetings?
Bam! ... I then realized that I hadn't made an intention statement and I had been focusing on what I did *not* want. I then understood why I was struggling and decided to start focusing on the exact outcome I wanted. What I really wanted was for the stock price to go up. I got too caught up in the details of how this should happen and thus created a platter full of struggle. I began applying the laws of prosperity and then sat back and waited. I even canceled the trip with the nasty guy I was about to go see.

Just a few short days later and pretty much out of nowhere, I was invited to speak at a retail stockbrokers' convention. I almost said "no" because I was more interested in speaking to stock analysts and fund managers than I was to retail brokers. Everything fell into place (it always does when you follow the Law of Least Effort) and I accepted the invitation. The best part was that I only had to fly to Arizona and I could play golf at the Boulders resort.

After my presentation, a young and friendly man walked up to me and asked if we could have dinner together. When I looked at his card, my jaw dropped open and I said, "Let's go!" The man, whom I will call "Tom," was an analyst for one of the biggest institutional brokerage firms in the world. During dinner, he asked hundreds of questions about the company, our strategy, the size of the market, and who our competitors were. He took copious notes; without my even realizing it, he was working on a research report for my company. (This was important because most brokers or fund managers would not buy my company's stock without a research report. Wall Street is extremely selective about the companies they issue research on.) Tom was quick to tell me that there were no guarantees and that I should not get my hopes up.

The following week, Tom called me and asked if I could go to New York and meet with him. I had a good feeling and this was a trip I was excited about taking. I was so excited, I asked my wife to come with me and we could make it a mini vacation. Neither of us will *ever* forget that trip to New York. At that time we were not making much money, since I had chosen to take a lot of shares of stock instead of a big salary. I rarely flew first class during this time and stayed in nice hotels but in basic rooms. The first thing that happened to us when we got to the airport is that we were randomly upgraded to first class. The gate agent liked that I was so upbeat at 5:00 in the morning and told me I was the first guy to make him smile that day. He then handed me our seat assignment with a smile on his face; I was delighted to see "Seats 2A and 2B" on the tickets. First class, baby!

When we got to the hotel, the desk clerk informed us they only had queen beds available. Instead of complaining, I smiled, winked at him, and said,"That's okay, maybe I'll get lucky tonight." My wife slugged me on the arm and we all laughed. The clerk then informed he did have one more room with a king bed in it, but it was a suite. Before I could answer, he told us it would be his pleasure to upgrade us. We walked into the suite and almost fainted! It was the Mickey Mantle Suite at the Broadway Sheraton in Manhattan and it was amazing. Not a bad trip so far, is it?

The next morning the phone rang, it was Tom, the analyst. He said he and his boss were outside our hotel and they wanted to see us right then. Although I had not finished getting ready, I figured I could close the door to the bedroom and use the huge suite as a meeting place. Both men were very impressed when they arrived and I must say, I felt like a player and my confidence was increased while speaking to Tom and his boss.

The meeting seemed to go well but neither of the two gentlemen would let on as to whether or not my company would receive the coverage we desired. That night while walking to dinner, in the middle of mid-town Manhattan, we ran right into Tom. Can you imagine? New York is both large and busy; the sidewalks are crowded with thousands of people. We were five blocks from our hotel and Tom was at least ten blocks from his office. Yet thanks to the Law of Attraction, we met face to face at the very same corner. He looked at us with a stunned expression and said, "Oh my God, I can't believe it's you!" He went on to say he had been trying to reach us all day because he needed to ask me a question before making a final decision on whether they would release their research report. They were trying to decide between two companies; they liked us better but because he couldn't reach me, they had decided to go with the other company.

I of course asked if it was too late, and then asked him what the question was. His question was whether or not I had any short-term plans to sell any of my personal shares (analysts do not like it when CEO's sell their stock). I told him "no." He immediately called his boss and had a quiet conversation. One minute later, Tom put his phone back in his pocket and said, "Today must be your lucky day! My boss was so blown away that I ran into you that he changed his mind and decided to issue our research report on your company!"

The next morning, the research report hit the wire service and suddenly millions of people knew all about my company. This is a true story and will hopefully affirm your belief in the Law of Least Effort. The moment I stopped focusing on what I did not want and began focusing on what I did want, I enabled the Law of Least Effort to deploy. Man, did it ever deploy! I no longer believe in coincidence; I attribute everything that appears to be a coincidence to the Law of Attraction and the Law of Least Effort.

Let's review the Law of Least Effort

- It will work when you focus on what you want.
- It will always lead you to precisely the right place at the right time.
- The clues left for you will be obvious if you are not struggling.
- Life should never be a struggle.
- When you force things, you are opposing the Law of Least Effort.

10

Putting it all together

Since the completion of this book, there has been more publicity than ever with regards to the Law of Attraction. A new book "The Secret has been released and it has already sold over 5.5 million copies!

The book continues to sell at a clip of 150,000 copies per week! This is astounding and warms my heart. For the first time in my life, the science of achievement has become a mainstream topic.

As one would expect, the media has now become fascinated with the Law of Attraction. Even Larry King has become a huge proponent and has interviewed several wealthy and successful individuals that participated in the making of both the movie and the book "The Secret"

With good press, comes bad press. I caution you to follow your heart and not blindly follow or listen to anyone ... INCLUDING ME!

The truth will ring clearly to your core and if you listen to the voice inside of you, you will know who is telling you the truth.

Selfishly, I ask that you carefully practice and follow all Six of The Irrefutable Laws of Prosperity. I believe if you examine each law, you will find both common sense and sound advice.

You need not believe in Quantum Physics, Universal Law or anything else for the Six Laws to make sense and to work for you.

I will now quickly review each law and attempt to tie them together for you:

1. The Law of Attraction—Simply stated, what you think about the most, you will draw into your life. There are several reasons for this, some involve Quantum Physics and the attractive qualities of vibrational energy and some involve good old fashioned common sense.

    From a common sense point of view, our thoughts formulate our beliefs. Right? The more we think about something, the more we develop it as belief. If you thought something to be untrue, why would you continue to think about it?

    We think about things we think are true or will come true and we form those thoughts into beliefs. Once a believe has developed, your conscious and sub-conscious mind will begin to find reasons to justify the belief.

    If your mind is working full time on justifying a belief you fed it, it will eventually prove you right. This has nothing to do with Quantum physics or energy.

    If you have read this book, you know I firmly believe this process to be far more powerful and driven by both science and nature. I believe thoughts become things and you will magnetize your destiny.

Either way ... guard your thoughts and focus only on the ones that serve you!

So, step one is simple. Decide on the type of life you want to live and drive your thoughts and energy toward that life. The Law of Attraction is always switched on, make sure the Law is working for you and not against you.

2. The Law of focus—I believe as a mammal we cannot control our thoughts. I am convinced that we CAN control our focus. My dog is also a mammal and also cannot control his thoughts.

What separates me from my dog is my ability to control my focus. If my dog Otis sees a bouncing ball, it is literally impossible for him not to focus on it. Even to his own demise! If that ball bounces on the freeway, Otis will still go after it.

As humans, our thoughts may take us in the direction of the ball but we sure as heck would not chase the ball into oncoming traffic.

Be a human and use your God given power to control your focus. If you do not like what you are thinking about, change you thought to something you do like.

If you are worried about money, don't think about money. Think about something that brings you joy. Remember, just as your thoughts become things, you also will get what you focus most on.

Focus on what you want. Never focus on what you don't want.

3. The Law of Emotion—This one is simple ... if you feel bad; you are focused on something bad. I use The Law of Emotion as an indicator as to what I am focusing on.

Many times we are not consciously aware of our thoughts or our current focus. We are however, always aware of how we are feeling. Feeling bad equals thinking bad, Feeling good equals thinking good.

Remember, you are attracting what you are focusing on. If your emotions tip you off to the fact that you are focusing on something bad, flip the switch and start thinking about something you want.

This morning my seven year old daughter was in an awful mood. She was bored, grumpy and unreasonable. When I asked her what was wrong, she told me she was upset because none of her friends could come over and play.

I made a couple of suggestions to make her feel better, only to watch her continue her downward spiral toward a terrible Saturday.

Quickly I asked what she was focusing on. Her answer was, "I am focusing on how mad I am that nobody can come over and play" I then asked her if her focus was making her feel good? Of course she said no.

I then asked her if she wanted to keep feeling bad. Of course she said no.

Finally, I asked her if there is anything she could focus on that would make her happy AND that she could control. Obviously, she cannot let her happiness be determined by things she cannot control.... like who can come play.

It was amazing to watch her run through a list in her mind of things that would make her happy. I listened as she listed activities and at the time qualified the activity to see if it was within her control.

Just the simple act of listing the activities she both could do and wanted to do, changed everything within five minutes, she was running around the yard playing with the Dogs.

In this case we used my daughter's emotion to determine and correct her focus. If it can work for a seven year old, it WILL work for you!

4. The Law of Gratitude—It is absolutely impossible to be grateful and unhappy at the same time. I promise. Go ahead, take a minute and think about something you are grateful for and then quickly check your emotional pulse.

The Law of Gratitude follows the Law of Emotion because Gratitude is the ultimate antidote for a lousy emotion. I have always said that gratitude is the turbo-charger of the law of attraction.

It is unlikely that you will ever obtain anything new or great without first being grateful for what you have. From a spiritual point of view, I believe the Universe wants to give more to those that are grateful. Just as I want to do more for my children when they are grateful.

Nobody wants to give an ungrateful child anything! If you put spirituality aside, just remember, feeling grateful makes you feel good! When you feel good, the Law of Attraction is working for you.

5. The Law of Intention—Now that you have your focus and emotions under control; it is time to CLEARLY state what you want. Be specific! State your intentions with confidence and repetition.

Intentions can also be referred to as affirmations. You must affirm what you intend to have constantly. When I am alone in the car or in my plane, I affirm the following simple sentence, "I am happy, healthy and wealthy" I will also vary the affirmation by stating, "I have happiness, health and wealth" and "I attract happiness, health and wealth."

Try saying that in traffic a couple hundred times. You will fell a profound shift in your energy.

Remember, if you do not ask for it, you cannot have it. State and affirm your intentions clearly and often.

6. The law of least effort—When I follow the first five laws, my life flows in amazing ways. Although I am not always certain exactly how things will play out, I trust in the Laws and follow the inner guidance I feel.

Sometimes the path is circuitous but it always seems to lead me to great places. When I find myself struggling or forcing things in my life, it is a sure sign that I have violated one of the first five laws.

I literally walk myself through them and can quickly figure out where I am off track. Usually, I am not focusing on what I want and in fact I will find that I am focusing on what I do NOT want.

This misguided focus, can quickly lead me off course. Once off course, I suddenly feel as if the tides have changed and I am forced to swim against the current.

The good news is that it is remarkably easy to catch this misguided focus and begin swimming with the current.

The law of least effort feels great when you let it work for you. When it is working against you, it is still a great indicator that you are not following one of the first five laws.

That summarizes all of the Six Irrefutable Laws of Prosperity. Now that you have read the book PLEASE practice the six laws! If at a minimum this book has increased your awareness and you begin catching yourself feeling bad, I believe you have begun your journey toward consistent happiness.

Conclusion

We hope you have found the Six Irrefutable Laws of Prosperity useful! We wish with all of our hearts that you will practice these laws on a daily basis. We know to the core of our souls that the practice of the Six Laws will have a dramatic and immediate impact on your life.

You will wonder why you were never taught to think this way as a child and you will rejoice at how simple it is to have a GREAT and prosperous life! The laws have never let us down and they do NOT discriminate for any reason. You should not argue with or question The Laws of Prosperity, just as you should not question the Law of Gravity. The only way you can fail, is to stop trusting in the Six Laws and to slip into your old habits.

Under stress, we humans will have a tendency to forget new things and slip back to our old and bad habits. Do not let this happen to you! When you feel worry, doubt, lack, fear or scarcity in your life ... PLEASE REOPEN THIS BOOK and reread these simple laws!

By the way ... The Six Laws work extremely well for children and teenagers as well! We are in the process of creating a series of books for children from first grade through high school. We are working on these books with well trained and well educated school teachers. Can you imagine how much better your children's lives will be by learning these success principles early? The concepts have been practiced with my own children and the results are absolutely amazing.

If you would like an early release of our books as they are completed, please go to our Web site at www.TrueSuccessNow.com and sign up for our mailing list. We also have a weekly ezine designed to provide weekly reminder and tips on the Six Irrefutable Laws of Prosperity.

Lastly, we are customizing our Six Laws for several vertical industries, beginning with the Real Estate and Mortgage industry. For those of you in the business, I think you will agree that there is a Macro contraction occurring. Focusing on the mass consciousness of this contraction will lead to a very sudden and severe decline in your business. We can teach you how to apply the Six Laws of Prosperity with some specific industry and internet tactics to help you Thrive will others are trying to survive. If you are interested in reading our Industry Specific books please email us at info@TrueSuccessNow.com.

We wish you all the best in the coming year and hope you feel free to contact us anytime for coaching or to chat!

Dan and Sophia Rawitch